HIKING COLORADO'S FRONT RANGE

Contact

Help Us Keep This Guide Up to Date

Every effort has been made by the author and editors to make this guide as accurate and useful as possible. However, many things can change after a guide is published—trails are rerouted, regulations change, techniques evolve, facilities come under new management, etc.

We would love to hear from you concerning your experiences with this guide and how you feel it could be improved and kept up to date. While we may not be able to respond to all comments and suggestions, we'll take them to heart and we'll also make certain to share them with the author. Please send your comments and suggestions to the following address:

> The Globe Pequot Press
> Reader Response/Editorial Department
> P.O. Box 480
> Guilford, CT 06437

Or you may e-mail us at:

> editorial@globe-pequot.com

Thanks for your input, and happy travels!

Hiking
COLORADO'S
FRONT RANGE

Fort Collins to Colorado Springs

Bob D'Antonio

FALCON®

GUILFORD, CONNECTICUT
HELENA, MONTANA
AN IMPRINT OF THE GLOBE PEQUOT PRESS

A FALCON GUIDE®

Copyright © 2003 by The Globe Pequot Press

Falcon and FalconGuide are registered trademarks of
The Globe Pequot Press.

All interior photos by the author
Maps created by Tony Moore © The Globe Pequot
Press

Library of Congress Cataloging-in-Publication Data
D'Antonio, Bob.
  Hiking Colorado's Front Range : Fort Collins to
Colorado Springs / Bob D'Antonio.
    p. cm. — (A FalconGuide)
  ISBN 0-7627-2208-8
    1. Hiking—Front Range (Colo. and Wyo.)—
Guidebooks. 2. Hiking—Colorado—Guidebooks. 3.
Front Range (Colo. and Wyo.)—Guidebooks. 4.
Colorado—Guidebooks. I. Title. II. Falcon guide.

GV199.42.F76 D36 2002
978.8'6—dc21

                            2002069307

Manufactured in the United States of America
First Edition/First Printing

Table of

Contents

Front Range Hikes

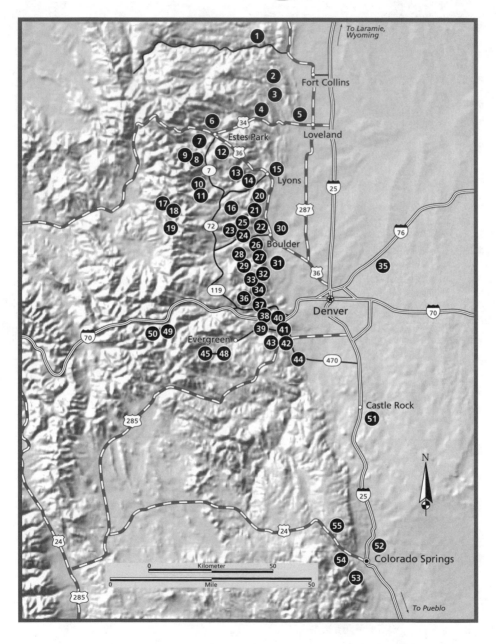

To Laramie, Wyoming

Fort Collins

Loveland

Estes Park

Lyons

Boulder

Denver

Evergreen

Castle Rock

Colorado Springs

To Pueblo

Kilometer

Mile

N

Denver, Foothills and Mountains

South of Denver/Colorado Springs Area

Map Legend

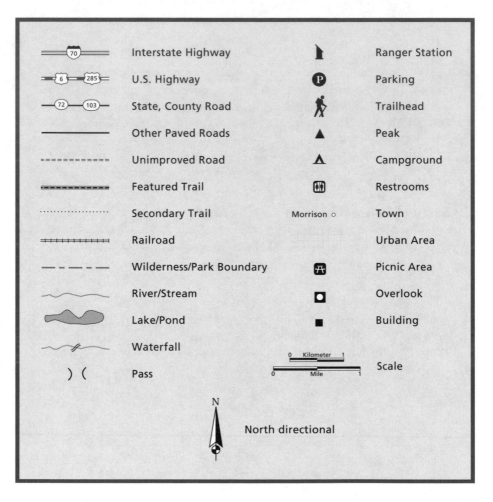

═══╣70╠═══	Interstate Highway
═╣6╠══╣285╠═	U.S. Highway
─╢72╟──╢103╟─	State, County Road
──────────	Other Paved Roads
============	Unimproved Road
▪▪▪▪▪▪▪▪▪▪	Featured Trail
··················	Secondary Trail
┼┼┼┼┼┼┼┼┼┼	Railroad
─ ─ ─ ─ ─	Wilderness/Park Boundary
～～～～～	River/Stream
(shape)	Lake/Pond
～～～	Waterfall
) (	Pass

◣	Ranger Station
🅿	Parking
🚶	Trailhead
▲	Peak
⌂	Campground
⌸	Restrooms
Morrison ○	Town
	Urban Area
🎪	Picnic Area
◉	Overlook
■	Building

Scale

0 Kilometer 1
0 Mile 1

N

North directional

Introduction

The Front Range of Colorado is an area that roughly extends from Fort Collins in the north to Pueblo in the south. This book explains in detail fifty-five hikes from Fort Collins to Colorado Springs. It is a spectacular area of low-lying plains, rounded foothills, towering mountain peaks, wide-open meadows, free-flowing rivers and streams, beautiful alpine lakes, glaciers, narrow gulches, tall rock walls, and views that extend in all directions. It is also an area of tremendous vertical relief: From the mile-high city of Denver you can travel west and in a mere 35 miles gain over 8,000 feet in altitude. At the heart of this great vertical topography are the southern Rocky Mountains and the Continental Divide. Colorado has the highest mountains in the Rocky Mountains and claims fifty-four summits over 14,000 feet high. The Continental Divide runs in a north-to-south direction near the center of the state and controls the flow of water from rivers and streams on both sides: West of the divide water flows to the Gulf of California; east into the Gulf of Mexico.

Between the plains and the high mountains are the foothills, a place of mixed forests, wide-open meadows filled with cacti, yuccas, wildflowers, various shrubs, piñon, junipers, ponderosas, aspens, tall cottonwoods, Douglas firs, and spruce trees. It is a place where myriad of animals call home. Mountain lions, elk, white-tailed deer, mule deer, prairie dogs, Abert squirrels, high-flying hawks, bald and golden eagles, prairie falcons, Canada geese, and other migratory birds can be found in this very diverse area; more than 960 species of animals call the open lands of the Front Range home. One can walk through most open areas and spot or hear one or many of these animals. Coyotes sing as they hunt at night; elk bugle in the fall looking for mates; bighorn sheep roam the high country and climb steep rock walls with sure-footed moves that would make any climber envious. Hawks and eagles fill the sky looking for food and cruising on thermals, diving and looking as though they don't have a care in the world.

There are five different life zones in the Front Range of Colorado. The Upper Sonoran is an area of high desert, filled with stunted piñon, small ponderosas, juniper trees, cacti, yuccas, and prairie grasses. It ranges from 4,000 to 6,000 feet above sea level. Next is the Transition Zone, an area that ranges from 6,000 to 8,000 feet above sea level. Tall ponderosas, Douglas firs, Gambel and mahogany oaks, various wildflowers, and the occasional lodgepole pine are found here. Above the Transition Zone is the Canadian Zone, an area that extends roughly from above 8,000 feet to nearly 10,000 feet in altitude. This zone is much cooler than the lower elevations and sees more precipitation.

Sugarloaf Mountain

Common trees include aspens, Engelmann spruce, and lodgepole pines. Wildflowers thrive in this zone, as do many animal species.

Next is the Hudsonian Zone, an area rising from 10,000 feet to above timberline, roughly around 11,000 feet above sea level. This zone is home to hardy species of trees and animals: Bristlecones, limber, and subalpine firs all live in this harsh environment and somehow cling to life in an area that is pounded by high winds and extreme weather. Last is the Arctic-Alpine Zone, which lies above timberline. This is an area where only the hardiest of plant and animal species can survive. When I travel above timberline I am amazed to find that tundra grasses, small stunted wildflowers, pikas, summering elk, and bighorn sheep somehow seem to thrive in the summer months at this harsh altitude. It is a place where I respect all living things for their tenacious will to survive. Winter can start as early as September and last well into July.

Very few places in the United States can lay claim to such a diverse physical environment. This is indeed a special area, and I feel that all the hikes in this book are special. From the riparian ecosystem of Barr Lake State Park to the snow-capped summit of Grays Peak and everything in between, one can seek solitude in these lands. You can hike along wild mountain streams and hear the sound of mountain water, a sound that will calm your heart and lighten your spirit. You can sit on top of high mountain peaks and look in all directions, feeling that you can see to forever. You can wander through the aspens in fall, seeing and hearing their gold leaves quaking in a soft breeze. You can hike on a narrow mountain trail under a canopy of tall pine trees and see wild animals in their natural environment, or fish high alpine lakes under towering rocky peaks and hear the sound of solitude. Believe me, that is a beautiful sound. But most of all, with a little bit of effort and with strong legs and lungs, you can experience the natural world of Colorado's Front Range. Hopefully this book will help you get there.

Climate

Colorado's Front Range is blessed with brilliant weather and sees almost 300 days of sunshine. You can hike in Colorado's Front Range year-round. Summer can be hot, but all you have to do to escape the heat is travel to the high country. Winters are mild, and in high snow years you can strap on a pair of skis or snowshoes and experience the quiet that only winter brings. Spring and fall are times of stable weather and moderate temperatures. Summer in the high country is absolutely beautiful, and you should make it a point to travel and experience the beauty of the high mountain peaks.

Hiking with Children

One of the greatest joys my wife and I have had is the time we have spent with our three children in the woods. Hiking is a wonderful family sport that can be enjoyed by the entire family. With that said, things can go wrong with children when you are out in the woods, and they can go wrong very fast. Be prepared! Take extra clothing, food, diapers, water, and a healthy sense of humor.

Day hikes and shorter ones are the best for introducing your child to the outdoors. Your child's age and fitness level will dictate how many miles you will travel in the woods. For toddlers, 1 to 4 miles will be just right. They are the hardest to travel with in the woods, and depending on how much or how long you want to carry them, your hike could be shorter. My son Jeremy had his own little backpack at the age of five and loved to carry his own food and water when we went into the woods. Older children travel at a faster rate and are strong enough to carry most of their gear. They require less attention and like to travel ahead of the adults, exploring on their own. Make sure the older children don't travel too far ahead and emphasize that they stay on the trail and wait for you at all trail junctions.

Younger children have a different agenda than most adults. They travel at a slower pace; they stop and check things out. Tree stumps, streams, butterflies, flowers, snow, and lakes are quite fascinating to their inquiring minds. They like to look at animals and bugs. Children will stop and sit down for no reason at all. They will ask a million questions. As a parent, enjoy your time with your children. Stop and answer all those questions. Sit with them on a log and treasure the time with your little ones in the woods; you won't regret it.

How to Use This Guide

This guide provides information on fifty-five hikes in the plains, foothills, and mountains of Colorado's Front Range. The hikes in this book range in length from 1 to 15 miles, with elevation gains as little as 100 feet to more than 3,000 feet. The trails vary from extremely rocky to flat and smooth. The hikes in this book start at an elevation of just over 5,000 feet and go up to 14,000 feet above sea level. The hikes run in a north-to-south direction, with Greyrock National Recreation Trail just north of Fort Collins as number 1 and Waldo Canyon just west of Colorado Springs as number 55.

Each hike description begins with the highlights of the hike, outlining the physical, historical, and other special attractions that you may find along the way. Information is then given about what season is best to do the hike, how long the hike is, and the difficulty of the hike. Following that, the maps that you will need, the entity that manages the area, trail conditions, and directions to the trailhead are all listed. Next are the key points along the trail, with mileages, followed by a detailed description of the hike.

A majority of the hikes in this book are day hikes and can easily be completed in a reasonable time frame. Almost all the hikes in this book could be turned into overnight excursions with the addition of a backpack, sleeping bag, tent, and other essentials. Make sure camping is allowed on the hike you are planning to do.

Read through the text and find the hike or hikes that best suit your needs. Distances are given for each hike and should be used as a reference point. Don't let the length of a hike stop you from doing that hike; go as far as you like on any given trail. If you are not up to completing a hike in this guide, turn around and return to the trailhead; come back another day. Just being outdoors and walking is enough for me.

Type of Trail

Suggested hikes have been categorized as follows:

Day hike: Best for a short excursion only, due to lack of either water or suitable camping sites.

Backpack: Best for backpacking with at least one or more nights in the backcountry. Many of the overnight hikes can be done as day hikes if you have the time and/or stamina.

Loop: Starts and finishes at the same trailhead with no (or very little) retracing of your steps. Sometimes the definition of a "loop" includes creative shapes (like a figure eight or lollipop) and a short walk on a dirt road to get you back to the trailhead.

Out-and-back: Traveling the same route coming and going.

Shuttle: A point-to-point trip that requires two vehicles (one left at each end of the trail) or a prearranged pickup at a designated time and place. One effective way to manage the logistical difficulties of shuttles is to arrange for a second party to start at the other end of the trail. The two parties then rendezvous at a predetermined time and place along the trail, trade keys, and drive to each other's home upon returning to the trailhead.

Difficulty Ratings

Difficulty ratings are inherently flawed: What's easy for you might be difficult for me. Still, such ratings serve as a general guide and give a useful approximation of a hike's challenge. Remember that ratings are not the final word, and that the most important factor is to be honest about your own fitness level when planning your trip. In this guidebook, difficulty ratings consider both how long and strenuous a hike is. Following are general guidelines for ratings:

Easy: Suitable for any hiker—young or old. Expect no serious elevation gain, hazards, or navigation problems.

Moderate: Suitable for hikers who have at least some experience and average fitness level. Likely includes some elevation change and may have places where the trail is faint.

Strenuous: Suitable only for experienced hikers with above average fitness level. Possible hazardous trail sections, navigation difficulties, and serious elevation change.

Trail Mileage

Measuring trail distances is an inexact science at best. In this guidebook most distances have been taken from map measurements and from in-the-field estimates. Most trail signs on Colorado's Front Range do not include distances, and when they do you can bet they are just somebody else's best guess. Keep in mind that distance is often less important than difficulty. A steep 2-mile climb on rocky tread can take longer than a 4-mile stroll through a gentle river valley. It may be helpful to note that most hikers average about 2 miles per hour and take into consideration that what matters is not how far you go, it's how much you enjoy your time out on the trail.

Maps

The maps in this book serve as a general guide only. Don't hit the trail without buying a better, more detailed map. There are a few choices when it comes to maps, and they are listed with each hike.

Elevation Charts

All hike descriptions include elevation charts. Use these profiles to get a general picture of how much elevation gain and loss a hike entails. The charts are not meant to be a detailed, foot-by-foot account of the route, but serve as a quick glimpse of the overall elevation change.

Backcountry Regulations

- Get a wilderness permit for all overnight use (see Appendix A).
- Camp only in appropriate places (see Zero Impact, below).
- Stay on trails (where possible) and don't create shortcuts.
- Dispose of human waste in a cat hole at least 200 feet from all water sources and campsites.
- Dispose of bathing and dishwater well away from water sources.
- Use camp stoves rather than cooking fires whenever possible.
- Carry out all trash. If you can pack it in, you can pack it out.
- Limit group size to ten or fewer.
- Suspend food out of reach of animals.
- Do not feed or in any way disturb the wildlife. Do not leave behind food scraps.
- Do not operate any mechanized vehicle in the wilderness.
- Do not destroy, deface, disturb, or remove from its natural setting any plant, rock, animal, or archaeological resource.
- Please read Zero Impact (below) for more details on minimizing impact on the wilderness.

Zero Impact

Going into a wild area is like visiting a famous museum. You obviously do not want to leave your mark on an art treasure in the museum. If everybody going through the museum left one little mark, the piece of art would be quickly destroyed—and of what value is a big building full of trashed art? The same goes for pristine wildlands. If we all left just one little mark on the landscape, the backcountry would soon be spoiled.

A wilderness can accommodate human use as long as everybody behaves. But a few thoughtless or uninformed visitors can ruin it for everybody who follows. All backcountry users have a responsibility to follow the rules of zero-impact camping.

Nowadays most wilderness users want to walk softly, but some aren't aware that they have poor manners. Often their actions are dictated by the outdated habits of a past generation of campers, who cut green boughs for evening shelters, built campfires with fire rings, and dug trenches around tents. In the 1950s, these practices may have been acceptable. But they leave long-lasting scars, and today such behavior is absolutely unacceptable.

Because wild places are becoming rare and the number of users is mushrooming, a new code of ethics is growing out of the necessity of coping with the unending waves of people who want a perfect backcountry experience. Today, we all must leave no clues that we were there. Enjoy the wild, but don't leave any trace of your visit.

THREE FALCON PRINCIPLES OF ZERO IMPACT
Leave with everything you brought in.
Leave no sign of your visit.
Leave the landscape as you found it.

Most of us know better than to litter—in or out of the backcountry. Be sure you leave nothing, regardless of how small it is, along the trail or at your campsite. This means you should pack out everything, including orange peels, flip tops, cigarette butts, and gum wrappers. Also, pick up any trash that others leave behind.

Follow the main trail. Avoid cutting switchbacks and walking on vegetation beside the trail. Don't pick up "souvenirs," such as rocks, antlers, or wildflowers. The next person wants to see them, too, and collecting such souvenirs violates many regulations.

Avoid making loud noises on the trail (unless you are in bear country) or in camp. Be courteous—remember that sound travels easily in the backcountry, especially across water.

Carry a lightweight trowel to bury human waste 6 to 8 inches deep at least 200 feet from any water source. Pack out used toilet paper.

Go without a campfire. Carry a stove for cooking and a flashlight, candle lantern, or headlamp for light. For emergencies, learn how to build a no-trace fire.

Camp in obviously used sites when they are available. Otherwise, camp and cook on durable surfaces such as bedrock, sand, gravel bars, or bare ground.

Practice zero impact principles—and put your ear to the ground and listen carefully. Thousands of people coming behind you are thanking you for your courtesy and good sense.

Details on these guidelines and recommendations of zero-impact principles for specific outdoor activities can be found in the FalconGuide *Leave No Trace*. Visit your local bookstore, go to the Web site www.falcon.com, or call The Globe Pequot Press at (800) 243–0495 to order a copy.

Backcountry Safety and Hazards

The Boy Scouts of America have been guided for decades by what is perhaps the single best piece of safety advice—Be prepared! For starters, this means carrying survival and first-aid materials, proper clothing, a compass, and a topographic map—and knowing how to use them.

Perhaps the second-best piece of safety advice is to tell somebody where you're going and when you plan to return. Pilots must file flight plans before every trip, and anybody venturing into a blank spot on the map should do the same. File your "flight plan" with a friend or relative before taking off.

Close behind your flight plan and being prepared with proper equipment is physical conditioning. Being fit not only makes wilderness travel more fun, it makes it safer. Here are a few more tips:

- Check the weather forecast. Be careful not to get caught at high altitude by a bad storm or along a stream in a flash flood. Watch cloud formations closely so you don't get stranded on a ridgeline during a lightning storm. Avoid traveling during prolonged periods of cold weather.
- Avoid traveling alone in the wilderness and keep your party together.
- Don't exhaust yourself or other members of your party by traveling too far or too fast. Let the slowest person set the pace.
- Study basic survival and first aid before leaving home.
- Before you leave for the trailhead, find out as much as you can about the route, especially the potential hazards.
- Don't wait until you're confused to look at your maps. Follow them as you go along, so you have a continual fix on your location.
- If you get lost, don't panic. Sit down and relax for a few minutes while you carefully check your topo map and take a compass reading. Confidently plan your next move. It's often smart to retrace your steps until you find familiar ground, even if you think it might lengthen your trip. Lots of people get temporarily lost in the wilderness and survive—usually by calmly and rationally dealing with the situation.
- Stay clear of all wild animals.
- Take a first-aid kit that includes, at a minimum, a sewing needle, snake-bite kit, aspirin, antibacterial ointment, antiseptic swabs, butterfly bandages, adhesive tape, adhesive strips, gauze pads, two triangular bandages, codeine tablets, two inflatable splints, moleskin for blisters, 3-inch gauze, CPR shield, rubber gloves, and lightweight first-aid instructions.

- Take a survival kit that includes, at a minimum, a compass, whistle, matches in a waterproof container, cigarette lighter, candle, signal mirror, flashlight, fire starter, aluminum foil, water purification tablets, space blanket, and flare.

Finally, don't forget that knowledge is the best defense against unexpected hazards. Read up on the latest in wilderness safety information in the FalconGuide *Wild Country Companion*.

Lightning: You Might Never Know What Hit You

Mountains are prone to sudden thunderstorms. If you get caught in a lightning storm, take special precautions. Remember,

- Lightning can travel ahead of a storm, so take cover before the storm hits.
- Don't try to make it back to your vehicle. It isn't worth the risk. Instead, seek shelter even if it's only a short way back to the trailhead. Lightning storms usually don't last long, and from a safe vantage point, you might enjoy the sights and sounds.
- Be especially careful not to get caught on a mountaintop or exposed ridge; under large, solitary trees; in the open; or near standing water.
- Seek shelter in a low-lying area, ideally in a stand of small, uniformly sized trees.
- Avoid anything that attracts lightning, like metal tent poles, graphite fishing rods, or pack frames.
- Crouch with both feet firmly on the ground.
- If you have a pack (without a metal frame) or a sleeping pad with you, put your feet on it for extra insulation against shock.
- Don't walk or huddle together. Instead, stay 50 feet apart, so if somebody gets hit by lightning, others in your party can give first aid.
- If you're in a tent, stay in your sleeping bag with your feet on your sleeping pad.

Hypothermia: The Silent Killer

Be aware of hypothermia—a condition in which the body's internal temperature drops below normal. It can lead to mental and physical collapse and death.

Hypothermia is caused by exposure to cold and is aggravated by wetness, wind, and exhaustion. The moment you begin to lose heat faster than your body produces it, you're suffering from exposure. Your body starts involuntary exercise, such as shivering, to stay warm and makes involuntary adjustments to preserve normal temperature in vital organs, restricting blood flow in the extremities. Both responses drain your energy reserves. The only way to stop the drain is to reduce the degree of exposure.

With full-blown hypothermia, as energy reserves are exhausted, cold blood reaches the brain, depriving you of good judgment and reasoning power. You won't be aware that this is happening. You lose control of your hands. Your internal temperature slides downward. Without treatment, this slide leads to stupor, collapse, and death.

To defend against hypothermia, stay dry. When clothes get wet, they lose about 90 percent of their insulating value. Wool loses relatively less heat; cotton, down, and some synthetics lose more. Choose rain clothes that cover the head, neck, body, and legs and provide good protection against wind-driven rain. Most hypothermia cases develop in air temperatures between 30 and 50 degrees, but hypothermia can develop in warmer temperatures.

If your party is exposed to wind, cold, and wet, watch yourself and others for uncontrollable fits of shivering; vague, slow, slurred speech; memory lapses; incoherence; immobile, fumbling hands; frequent stumbling or a lurching gait; drowsiness; apparent exhaustion; and inability to get up after a rest. When a member of your party has hypothermia, he or she may deny any problem. Believe the symptoms, not the victim. Even mild symptoms demand the following treatment:

- Get the victim out of the wind and rain.
- Strip off all wet clothes.
- If the victim is only mildly impaired, give him or her warm drinks. Then get the victim in warm clothes and a warm sleeping bag. Place well-wrapped water bottles filled with heated water close to the victim.
- If the victim is badly impaired, attempt to keep him or her awake. Put the victim in a sleeping bag with another person—both naked. If you have a double bag, put two warm people in with the victim.

Fording Rivers

Early summer hiking in the mountains of Colorado's Front Range may involve crossing streams swollen with runoff. When done correctly and carefully, crossing a big river can be safe, but you must know your limits.

Know those cases where you simply should turn back. Even if only one member of your party (such as a child) might not be able to follow larger, stronger members, you might not want to try a risky ford. Never be embarrassed by being too cautious.

One key to safely fording rivers is confidence. If you aren't a strong swimmer, you should be. This not only allows you to safely get across a river that is a little deeper and stronger than you thought, but it gives you the confidence to avoid panic. Just like getting lost, panic can easily make the situation worse.

Practice builds confidence. Find a warm-water river near your home and carefully practice crossing it both with a pack and without. You can also start with a smaller stream and work up to a major river. After you've become a strong swimmer, get used to swimming in the current.

When you get to the ford, carefully assess the situation. Don't automatically cross at the point where the trail comes to the stream and head on a straight line for the marker on the other side. A mountain river can change every spring during high runoff, so a ford that was safe last year might be too deep this year. Study upstream and downstream and look for a place where the stream widens and the water is not over waist deep on the shortest member of your party. The tail end of an island is usually a good place, as is a long riffle. The inside of a meander sometimes makes a safe ford, but in other cases a long, shallow section can be followed by a short, deep section next to the outside of the bend where the current picks up speed and carves out a deep channel.

Before starting any serious ford, make sure your matches, camera, billfold, clothes, sleeping bag, and other items you must keep dry are in watertight bags.

On Colorado's Front Range, most streams are cold, so have dry clothes ready when you get to the other side to minimize the risk of hypothermia, especially on a cold, rainy day.

Minimize the amount of time you spend in the water, but don't rush across. Instead, go slowly and deliberately, taking one step at a time, being careful to get each foot securely planted before lifting the other foot. Take a 45-degree angle instead of going straight across, following a riffle line if possible.

Don't ford with bare feet. Wear hiking boots without the socks, sneakers, or tightly strapped sandals. In an emergency, wool socks pulled over rubber soles provide a good grip on the slippery rock.

Keep sideways to the current. Turning upstream or downstream increases the current's force.

In some cases, two or three people can cross together, locking forearms, with the strongest person on the upstream side.

When in mountainous terrain, and if you have a choice, ford in the early morning when the stream isn't as deep. The cool evening temperatures slow snow melt and reduce the water flow into the rivers.

On small streams, a sturdy walking stick used on the upstream side for balance helps prevent a fall, but in a major river with a fast current, a walking stick offers little help.

Loosen the belt and straps on your pack. If you fall or get washed downstream, a waterlogged pack can anchor you to the bottom, so you must be able to easily release your pack.

If you're 6' 4" and a strong swimmer, you might feel secure crossing a big river, but you might have children or smaller hikers in your party. In this case, the strongest person can cross first and string a line across the river to aid those who follow. This line (with the help of a carabiner) can also be used to float packs across instead of taking the chance of a waterlogged pack dragging you under. (If you knew about the ford in advance, you could pack a lightweight rubber raft or inner tube for this purpose.) Depending on your size and strength, you might also want to carry children.

Be prepared for the worst. Sometimes circumstances arise where you simply must cross instead of going back, even though the ford looks dangerous. Also, you can underestimate the depth of the channel or strength of the current, especially after a thunderstorm when a muddy river hides its true depth. In these cases, whether you like it or not, you might be swimming. If this happens, don't panic, and do not try to swim directly across. Instead, pick a long angle and gradually cross to the other side, taking as much as 100 yards or more to finally get across. If your pack starts to drag you down, release it immediately, even if you have to abandon it. If you lose control and get washed downstream, go feet first, so you don't hit your head on rocks or logs.

Be sure to report any dangerous ford to a ranger as soon as you finish your trip.

Be Mountain Lion Alert

You're sure to see plenty of deer along Colorado's Front Range, which means mountain lions probably aren't far away. Cougars feed on deer and elk, and the rugged, rocky areas along Colorado's Front Range constitute some of the best cougar habitat in the West. Although many people consider themselves lucky indeed to see a mountain lion in the wild, the big cats—nature's perfect predator—are potentially dangerous. Attacks on humans are extremely rare, but it's wise to educate yourself before heading into mountain lion habitat.

Safety guidelines for traveling in mountain lion country: To stay as safe as possible when hiking in mountain lion country, follow this advice:
- Travel with a friend or group and stay together.
- Don't let small children wander away by themselves.
- Don't let pets run unleashed.
- Avoid hiking at dawn and dusk when mountain lions are most active.
- Know how to behave if you encounter a mountain lion.

What to do if you encounter a mountain lion: In the vast majority of mountain lion encounters, these animals exhibit avoidance, indifference, or curiosity that never results in human injury. But it is natural to be alarmed if you have an encounter of any kind. Try to keep your cool and consider the following:

Recognize threatening mountain lion behavior. A few cues may help you gauge the risk of attack. If a mountain lion is more than 50 yards away, and it directs its attention to you, it may be only curious. This situation represents only a slight risk for adults but a more serious risk to unaccompanied children. At this point, you should move away, while keeping the animal in your peripheral vision. Also, look for rocks, sticks, or something to use as a weapon, just in case. If a mountain lion is crouched and staring at you less than 50 yards away, it may be assessing the chances of a successful attack. If this behavior continues, the risk of attack may be high.

Do not approach a mountain lion. Give the animal the opportunity to move on. Slowly back away, but maintain eye contact if close. Mountain lions are not known to attack humans to defend young or a kill, but they have been reported to "charge" in rare instances and may want to stay in the area. It's best to choose another route or time to hike through the area.

Do not run from a mountain lion. Running may stimulate a predatory response.

Make noise. If you encounter a mountain lion, be vocal and talk or yell loudly and regularly. Try not to panic. Shout to make others in the area aware of the situation.

Maintain eye contact. Eye contact presents a challenge to the mountain lion, showing you are aware of its presence. Eye contact also helps you know where it is. However, if the behavior of the mountain lion is not threatening (if it is, for example, grooming or periodically looking away), maintain visual contact through your peripheral vision and move away.

Appear larger than you are. Raise your arms above your head and make steady waving motions. Raise your jacket or another object above your head. Do not bend over, as this will make you appear smaller and more "prey-like."

If you are with small children, pick them up. Bring children close to you, maintain eye contact with the mountain lion, and pull the children up without bending over. If you are with other children or adults, band together.

Defend yourself and others. If attacked, fight back. Try to remain standing. Do not feign death. Pick up a branch or rock; pull out a knife, pepper spray, or other deterrent device. Individuals have fended off mountain lions with rocks, tree limbs, and even cameras. Keep in mind this is a last effort and defending pets is not recommended.

Respect any warning signs posted by agencies.

Teach others in your group how to behave in case of a mountain lion encounter.

Report encounters. Record your location and the details of any encounter and notify the nearest land owner or land-managing agency. The land management agency (federal, state, or county) may want to visit the site and, if appropriate, post education/warning signs. Fish and wildlife agencies should also be notified because they record and track such encounters. If physical injury occurs, it is important to leave the area and not disturb the site of attack. Mountain lions that have attacked people must be killed, and an undisturbed site is critical for effectively locating the dangerous mountain lion.

See the FalconGuide *Mountain Lion Alert* for more details and tips for safe outdoor recreation in mountain lion country.

Be Bear Aware

The first step of any hike in bear country is an attitude adjustment. Being prepared for bears doesn't only mean having the right equipment. It also means having the right information. Black bears along Colorado's Front Range do not as a rule attack humans, but they may pose a danger if you handle your food improperly. At the very least, letting a bear get human food is like contributing—directly—to the eventual destruction of that bear. Think of proper bear etiquette as protecting the bears as much as yourself.

Camping in Bear Country

Staying overnight in bear country is not dangerous, but the presence of food, cooking, and garbage adds an additional risk to your trip. You are also in bear country at night when bears are usually most active. Following a few basic practices greatly minimizes the chance of encounter.

To be as safe as possible, store everything that has any food smell. Zip-locked bags are perfect for reducing food smell and help keep food from spilling on your pack, clothing, or other gear. If you spilled something on your clothes, change into other clothes for sleeping and hang clothes with food smells with the food and garbage. If you take them into the tent, you aren't separating your sleeping area from food smells. Try to keep food odors off your pack, but if you fail, put the food bag inside and hang the pack.

Be sure to finalize your food storage plans before it gets dark. It's not only difficult to store food after darkness falls, it's easier to forget some juicy morsel on the ground. Store food in airtight, sturdy, waterproof bags to prevent food odors from circulating throughout the forest. You can purchase dry bags at most outdoor specialty stores, but you can get by with a trash compactor bag. Don't use regular garbage bags because they can break easily.

See the diagrams that follow for different ways to hang a bear bag. If you have two bags to hang, divide your food into two equal sacks. Use a stone to toss the end of a piece of nylon cord (parachute cord is fine; under most circumstances there is no need for the heavier stuff) over the limb well out from the trunk, then tie half your food to the end. Pull the food up to the limb, then tie your remaining food sack onto the cord as high as you can reach. Stuff the excess cord into the food sack, then use a stick to push the second sack several feet higher than your head. The first sack will act as a counterweight and descend a few feet, but it should remain at least as high as the second sack. In the morning, use a stick to pull down one of the sacks.

Don't get paranoid about the types of food you bring—all food has some smell. By consciously reducing the number of dishes (pack out all food scraps) and the amount of packaging and consuming everything on your plate, as well as paying careful attention to storage, you will make your backpacking culinary

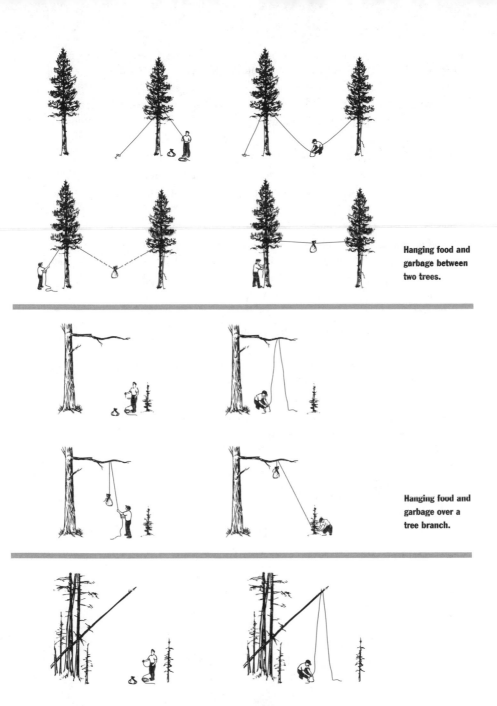

Hanging food and garbage between two trees.

Hanging food and garbage over a tree branch.

Hanging food and garbage over a leaning tree.

experience not only more enjoyable and hassle free for yourself, but also more bear proof.

Read the FalconGuide *Bear Aware* by Bill Schneider for complete information on camping in bear country.

Remember Rattlesnakes

Rattlesnakes strike humans only out of self-defense, when they're startled or otherwise afraid. The solution, of course, is to avoid scaring them. Look where you place your feet and hands when hiking in rattlesnake country (which includes most of the trails in *Hiking Colorado's Front Range*, but especially those at lower, warmer elevations).

If you do encounter a rattlesnake, slowly back away and give it a chance to go away. Almost invariably it will seize the opportunity and slither away. If it doesn't, simply give the snake a wide berth and leave well enough alone. Do not throw rocks or sticks at it.

If bitten by a rattlesnake, don't panic. Rattlesnake bites are rarely fatal to healthy adults. Use a snake-bite kit immediately to extract as much of the venom as possible. (It may actually be a "dry bite" in which no venom is delivered—intended only to frighten you.) Do not run or otherwise speed up your circulation, as that increases the spread of the venom in your bloodstream. Keep the bite site lower than your heart to slow the spread of venom. Seek medical attention as soon as possible.

Fort Collins
AREA

1

Greyrock National Recreation Trail

Highlights: *This is a beautiful hike up into some very wild country high above the Cache la Poudre River. Wildlife, views, and a steep grunt up a narrow gulch to a beautiful open meadow are the highlights on this hike. Wildflowers abound in Greyrock Meadow during the early summer months.*

Season: Year-round depending on snowfall.
Distance: 5.9-mile loop.
Difficulty: Moderate to strenuous.

Maps: Trails Illustrated/Cache la Poudre/Big Thompson #101.
Management: Roosevelt National Forest.
Trail conditions: The trail is rocky.

Finding the trailhead: From Fort Collins travel north on U.S. Highway 287 to Colorado Highway 14. Travel west on CO 14 up Poudre Canyon for 8.2 miles to the Greyrock National Recreation trailhead and parking on the left.

Key points:
0.6 The trail forks.
1.3 Small creek crossing.
2.2 Trail junction and Greyrock Mountain.
2.9 Greyrock Meadow.
3.5 Overlook.
5.2 Trail junction.
5.9 Parking area.

The hike: From the parking area drop down the steps and cross CO 14. Use caution. Follow the trail across the bridge and arrive at the start of the Greyrock National Recreation Trail. Go left up along the Cache la Poudre River through thickets, willows, tall grasses, yuccas, and ponderosa pines. The

Greyrock National Recreation Trail

To Fort Collins

Cache la Poudre River

N

Kilometer

Mile

0

0

Greyrock Mountain
7,613 ft.

Greyrock Meadow

Greyrock National
Recreation Trail
946

Greyrock Meadow Trail

Hewlett Gulch

START/END

P

14

Poudre
Park

Poudre Park
Picnic Ground

trail climbs at a nice grade and goes to the right up a narrow gulch away from the river. Continue climbing through the trees up to a trail junction at around the 0.6-mile mark. The Greyrock Trail goes to the right and the Greyrock Meadow Trail goes to the left. This hike takes the Greyrock Trail and heads up into a very narrow gulch. Follow the tight trail through a rocky section climbing a steep grade. Large rocks cover the steep hillsides of the trail, as do beautiful ponderosa pines and various wildflowers. The trail climbs a short distance to the left then climbs back right, up to a small seasonal creek. Cross the creek and climb several short switchbacks with the trail now on the right of the drainage. Aspen trees appear and blend in nicely with the tall pine trees. The trail becomes level and travels up past several large ponderosa trees. At around the 1.7-mile mark the trail switches back and forth over the gulch and then makes a left away from the gulch across a steep hillside. Several burned trees line the trail, probably the victims of a lightning strike. There are excellent views to the south, and you can look down the gulch and see the substantial elevation gain you have made. Reach a cluster of rocks, enjoy the views, and take a break. Follow the trail up through several rocks near the trail. Catch a glimpse of Greyrock Mountain's granite walls and arrive at a trail junction in an open meadow. Go left on the Greyrock Meadow Trail through a beautiful meadow and then back into the trees. The trail drops down on rocky tread into the wide, beautiful Greyrock Meadow. It then slices across the meadow, with large, granite rocks clinging to the steep hillsides. There is a great view back to Greyrock Mountain, and the meadow is filled with wildflowers during the summer months. The trail goes left into the trees and climbs through several rocky sections to a ridge. The trail pops out of the trees and begins a steep descent down an open hillside. The trail takes several long switchbacks and then plunges into a narrow gulch. Follow the trail into the gulch and drainage. Willows, aspens, and wildflowers grow close to the drainage and are quite a contrast to the steep hill you just descended. Arrive back at a familiar trail junction and continue straight to the footbridge. Cross the bridge and highway and climb the step back to the parking area.

2

Arthur's Rock

Highlights: *Wonderful hiking in a beautiful state park just west of Fort Collins. This loop takes you up to Arthur's Rock, traveling over beautiful flower-filled hills, with views to the east of Horsetooth Reservoir, south to Horsetooth Mountain Park, and east to the plains. A great wildlife hike and a good place to bring the family and enjoy all the activities this park has to offer.*

Season: Year-round.
Distance: 1.8 miles one way.
Difficulty: Moderate.

Maps: USGS Horsetooth Reservoir/Lory State Park Map.
Management: Colorado State Parks.
Trail conditions: The trail is rocky.

Finding the trailhead: Head north on U.S. Highway 287 from Fort Collins, following the signs for Lory State Park. About 5 miles north of Fort Collins and just past the town of Laporte, turn left on County Road 54E. Getting to the park is half the fun. Look for County Road 25E. Go left on CR 25E cutting to the left. Follow CR 25E to County Road 23. Go right on CR 23 to Country Road 25G leading into Lory State Park. Pay the $5.00 entrance fee and travel 2.0 miles to Arthur's Rock Trailhead and parking area. The hike starts here.

Key points:
0.3 Overlook Trail junction.
1.3 Overlook on the right.
1.7 Junction with Timber Trail.
1.8 Summit of Arthur's Rock.

The hike: From the trailhead go west past the restrooms and (very informative) kiosk on the Arthur's Rock Trail. Cross a wood footbridge and head left across another footbridge and into a narrow gulch. Follow the narrow, rocky trail up through the mouth of the gulch. The trail climbs several switchbacks, gaining altitude, and comes to a junction with the Overlook Trail in an open meadow. Wildflowers, tall grass, ponderosas, a great view of Arthur's Rock, and a cluster of cottonwoods on the right all add to the natural beauty of this wonderful spot. Continue straight on the Arthur's Rock Trail through the meadow to a trail junction at the 0.6-mile mark. Continue straight into the ponderosas and enjoy beautiful hiking under a canopy of these stately trees. The trail comes out of the trees, crosses a seasonal drainage, and then climbs

Arthur's Rock

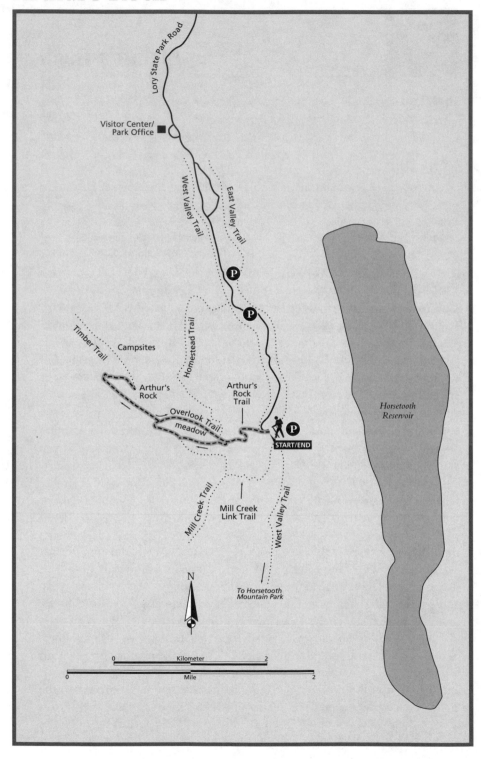

Lory State Park Road

Visitor Center/
Park Office

West Valley Trail

East Valley Trail

Ⓟ

Ⓟ

Timber Trail

Campsites

Homestead Trail

Arthur's
Rock

Arthur's
Rock
Trail

Overlook Trail

meadow

Ⓟ

START/END

Mill Creek Trail

Mill Creek
Link Trail

West Valley Trail

Horsetooth
Reservoir

N

To Horsetooth
Mountain Park

0	Kilometer	2
0	Mile	2

steeply up the side of an open hill to an overlook at the 1.3-mile mark. Go right for great views of Horsetooth Reservoir and the plains. Follow the trail along the base of Arthur's Rock on narrow tread; yuccas and cacti grow on the steep, sunny slope on the left. The trail climbs rapidly and cuts past a tall, pointed boulder and through a narrow passage up to a junction with the Timber Trail. Reach the Timber Trail at the 1.7-mile mark and take a short break to soak in the views. To the east and running in a north and south direction, sandstone hogbacks are visible and reveal movements of the Earth millions of years ago. Two of the Earth's plates moved in an east and west direction. Where they hit each other the edges of the plates were pushed upward from deep in the Earth's core. Millions of years later, and with the help of wind, sun, snow, and rain, what was once deep underground now lies exposed. Go right and follow the trail down to the east. Then go left up a steep, rock-filled gully and gain a flat area and the top of Arthur's Rock. Enjoy the spectacular views to the north, east, and south. Use caution on the top of the rocks and limit the amount of scrambling you do on these steep rocks with big dropoffs. Retrace your route back to the overlook at the 1.3-mile mark. For a different return go left past the sign and drop down the Overlook Trail. The trail drops at a rapid rate and soon comes to a junction with the Homestead Trail. Continue down on the Overlook Trail, cross a small drainage, and meet the Arthur's Rock Trail. Go left on the Arthur's Rock Trail for 0.3 mile and arrive back at the trailhead.

3

Horsetooth Falls Loop

Highlights: *A beautiful hike up to a cascading waterfall on a trail through open hills, narrow gulches, open meadows, and rock-lined ridges. The best time of the year to do the hike is late spring when the wildflowers are blooming and the falls are quite impressive with water from the spring runoff.*

Season: Year-round. Best in late spring.
Distance: 3.4-mile loop.
Difficulty: Moderate.
Maps: USGS Horsetooth Reservoir/ Horsetooth Mountain Park.

Management: Larimer County Parks and Open Space.
Trail conditions: The trail is rocky.

Finding the trailhead: From U.S. Highway 287 and Harmony Avenue in Fort Collins go west on Harmony Avenue (County Road 38E) for 8.7 miles to the entrance of Horsetooth Mountain Park, the trailhead, and parking. Pay the $6.00 park admission fee.

Key points:
0.4 Horsetooth Falls Trail.
1.3 Horsetooth Falls.
1.8 Soderberg Trail junction.
2.6 Junction with Horsetooth Rock Trail.
2.7 Junction with Audra Culver Trail.
2.9 Hiker's trail.
3.0 Junction with the Horsetooth Falls Trail.
3.4 Back at the trailhead.

The hike: Grab a Horsetooth Falls Discovery Trail map from the kiosk. This is a great map to have; it explains the geology, wildlife, and history of the area. Head to the north and past the last picnic area to reach the start of the Soderberg Trail. Go through the gate and angle to the right on a narrow trail. Climb up past the first interpretive post and reach an open hillside. Head north to a lone ponderosa tree on the right and a junction with the Horsetooth Falls Trail. Go right on the Horsetooth Falls Trail and drop down past thickets, yuccas, and scrub oak to a narrow gulch. Look north on the steep hillside for mule deer, which like the grass-covered hillside. Head west up the gulch to a wood footbridge across Spring Creek. Climb steeply up wood and rock steps to a junction with the Spring Creek Trail at the 1.2-mile mark. Go left

Horsetooth Falls Loop

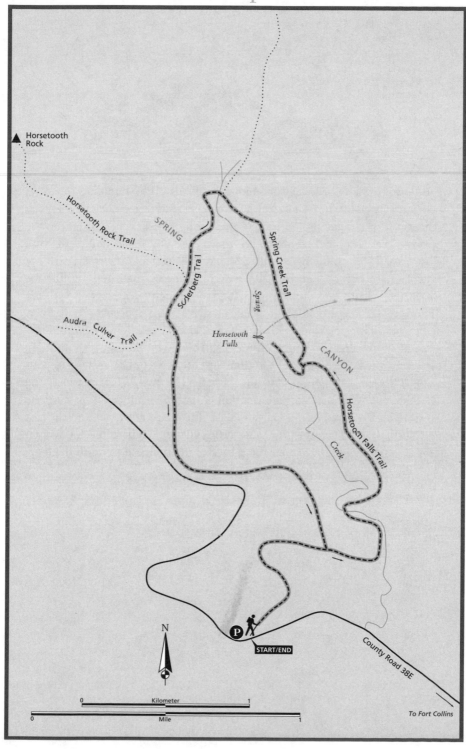

Horsetooth Rock

Horsetooth Rock Trail

SPRING

Soderberg Trail

Spring Creek Trail

Spring

Audra Culver Trail

Horsetooth Falls

CANYON

Horsetooth Falls Trail

Creek

N

P START/END

County Road 38E

To Fort Collins

Kilometer
0   1

Mile
0   1

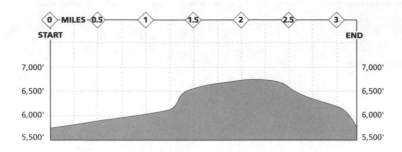

and down to the falls. Relax and enjoy the sounds of the tumbling waters. A bench is located off the trail and makes a great place to hang out and enjoy the scenery. Turn around and go back to the Spring Creek Trail. Go left up the Spring Creek Trail and climb steeply above the falls. Respect all of the trail closures and stay on the main trail. Reach a level area and traverse across the side of a steep hill covered with tall ponderosas, yuccas, cacti, and wildflowers. Reach the seventh interpretive sign. Continue straight to a junction with the Soderberg Trail. At around the 1.8-mile mark reach the Soderberg Trail. Relax at this beautiful spot. The cool waters of Spring Creek flow by, wildflowers grow along the creekside, and tall rocks surround you on the steep hillsides. Go left on the Soderberg Trail and climb up through a beautiful stand of ponderosas. Reach an open meadow on the left. The trail becomes wider, and stands of young ponderosas line the trail. Climb to a hill point, passing the Horsetooth Rock and Audra Culver Trails. There are great views to the east and north. Take the hiker's trail that drops steeply to the Horsetooth Falls Trail. Go right and retrace your route back to the trailhead to finish the loop.

4 Dome Mountain Trail

Highlights: *A strenuous hike up to the summit of Sheep Mountain, (8,450 feet) high above the Big Thompson River and Canyon. The trail is well marked with mileage markers and informative signs pointing out information on plant life, erosions, and geology.*

Season: April to November.
Distance: 4.5 miles one way.
Difficulty: Moderate to strenuous.
Maps: Trails Illustrated Cache la Poudre–Big Thompson #101.

Management: Roosevelt National Forest and the City of Loveland.
Trail conditions: The trail surface varies between very smooth in some sections to extremely rocky in others.

Finding the trailhead: From the junction of U.S. Highway 287 and U.S. Highway 34 in Loveland, travel west on US 34 for 14 miles into Big Thompson Canyon to the Dome Mountain Trailhead on the left. The hike starts at a gate near the restrooms.

Key points:
- 0.2 Go left.
- 0.4 Go left.
- 0.6 Talus slope.
- 1.0 Mile marker.
- 2.0 Mile marker.
- 2.5 Natural rock corridor.
- 2.9 Spring.
- 3.0 Mile marker.
- 3.5 Aspen forest.
- 4.0 Mile marker.
- 4.5 Sheep Mountain.

The hike: From the parking area follow the road up past a gate to a sign pointing to the summit trail. Make a quick left and go up to a second sign near a large pipe on the left. Go left again here; the trail becomes narrow as it clings to the side of a steep hill. Begin a steep climb to where the trail cuts across a talus slope. Read the first of many informative signs that are located along the trail. This section of the trail travels through a forest of beautiful ponderosa pines and the occasional Douglas fir. Along the trail pointed yuccas and prickly pear cacti grow alongside delicate blooming wildflowers. The trail switches

Dome Mountain Trail

To Estes Park

Drake

34

To Loveland

Cedar Cove

Big Thompson River

START/END

P

Dome Mountain Trail

Sheep Mountain
8,450 ft.

summit trail

N

Kilometer

Mile

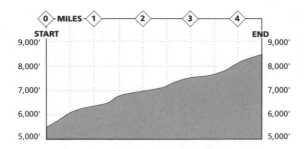

back steeply in a west-to-east direction, with nice views in both directions. Soon you arrive at the 1.0-mile marker, with open views to the east. The trail becomes quite steep as you continue to climb high above a narrow gulch that is down and to the left. The terrain stays rocky and continues to switchback up and up. Arrive at the 2.0-mile marker and begin the steepest section of the hike. The trail becomes quite narrow and very rocky as it travels through a

beautiful forest of mature ponderosa pines and weird rock formations. Slide through a natural
rock corridor and begin a slight
descent to a spring on the right
just before the 3.0-mile marker.
This is a good spot for a rest. At
the 3.0-mile marker the trail stays
fairly level and actually drops a
bit into a beautiful aspen forest
with a small drainage. What a
relief from all that climbing!
Enjoy nice hiking through the
aspen with views to the north and
west of Sheep Mountain. Arrive
at the 4.0-mile marker and cruise
up through the rocks to the summit of Sheep Mountain. Enjoy
views to the north and of
Loveland and the plains to the
east. After a well-deserved rest,
retrace your route back to the
trailhead.

Aspens, Dome Mountain Trail

5 Devil's Backbone Nature Trail

Highlights: *A nice family hike along the base of the Devil's Backbone just west of Loveland.*

Season: Year-round.
Distance: 2.7-mile loop.
Difficulty: Easy.
Maps: Larimer County, CO USGS, and Larimer County Open Space/Devil's Backbone.

Management: Larimer County Parks and Open Lands.
Trail conditions: The trail is smooth.

Finding the trailhead: From the intersection of U.S. Highway 287 and U.S. Highway 34 in Loveland, go west on US 34 for 4.8 miles to Glade Road. Turn right on Glade Road and make an immediate right turn on Wild Lane. Travel 0.3 mile on Wild Lane to the Devil's Backbone Trailhead and parking.

Key points:
0.3 Wood footbridges.
0.5 The trail forks.
1.3 The trail forks.
1.5 The Keyhole.
2.2 Trail junction.
2.7 Back at the parking area.

The hike: From the parking area travel north up to the kiosk. Grab a Devil's Backbone Nature Trail map. The map explains local history, geology, flora, and wildlife surrounding the Devil's Backbone area. Past the kiosk the trail follows a road leading to the Wild Lane Bed and Breakfast. Go right just before the bed-and-breakfast, following the sign for the Devil's Backbone Trail up to a gate. Stay right of the gate and curve around the side of a small hill with an

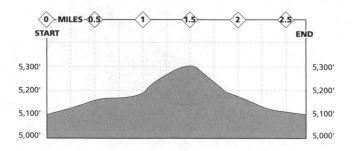

Devil's Backbone Nature Trail

The Keyhole —

Devil's Backbone Nature Trail

To Estes Park

34

Wild

Lane

P

START/END

N

To Loveland

| 0 | Kilometer | 1 |
| 0 | Mile | 1 |

Cacti, Devil's Backbone

irrigation ditch on your left and a house down to the right. Cross two wood footbridges at the 0.3-mile point and climb a small hill toward a trail junction. There are good views to the north, and in the early summer months yuccas, lupines, and other wildflowers bloom on the east-facing hill. Continue north. Arrive at the trail junction; for this hike go right. The trail travels through a nice area of mahogany oak, cacti, and hills filled with yuccas. At around the 1.0-mile mark a good view of Devil's Backbone can be seen to the west. Continue north up to a trail junction at the 1.3-mile mark where a new trail and loop continue to the north and east. For this hike, go left and angle back to the south and up toward the Keyhole (a keyhole-shaped rock formation caused by erosion). Arrive at the Keyhole and a metal post marked 6. Time to bring out the map and read about how the Keyhole was formed. Follow the trail along Devil's Backbone, keeping your map handy for quick reference. Reach a metal post marked 5 at the 1.7-mile mark. Learn who used to roam these lands millions of years ago. The trail crests a small hill at the 1.8-mile mark and offers great views to the north, south, and east. Large yuccas line the trail and tall prairie grass fills the open hillsides as you continue in a southerly direction back to the trailhead. At the 2.0-mile mark reach a metal post marked 3 and read the map. The trail makes a slight decline and you soon arrive at a familiar trail junction. Go right and retrace your route back to the trailhead and the end of the hike.

Estes Park/
LYONS AREA

6

Gem Lake Trail

Highlights: *A great family hike up to a small gem of a lake tucked neatly below small granite outcrops. This is a great little excursion for hikers of all abilities. Pack a lunch, bring the whole family, and enjoy this gem of a hike.*

Season: April to November.
Distance: 1.8 miles one way.
Difficulty: Moderate.
Maps: Trails Illustrated Rocky Mountain National Park #200.

Management: Rocky Mountain National Park.
Trail conditions: This is a well-used trail with mostly smooth tread.

Finding the trailhead: From Estes Park take MacGregor Avenue north for 0.8 mile, passing the Stanley Hotel. Go right at the gate leading into the road through the MacGregor Ranch up to the Twin Owl Trailhead and parking area.

Key points:

0.8 Devil's Gulch Trail junction.
1.8 Gem Lake.

The hike: This is a very popular trailhead and parking area for hikers and climbers. Arrive early in the morning during the summer months to secure a parking space. The hike starts near the restrooms below the towering cliffs of the Twin Owl formations. When looking at the cliffs from the south, the high rock walls resemble two perched owls. Access the trail near the restrooms and begin hiking through a beautiful, small aspen forest. Several climber-accessible trails shoot off to the left and up to the popular granite cliffs. The trail climbs up past the aspen and into open views and ponderosa pines. Looking west into Rocky Mountain National Park, you can see several high peaks, with Longs Peak being the most impressive and dominant at 14,255 feet above sea level. Several large boulders lie along the trail and are very popular with climbers

Gem Lake Trail

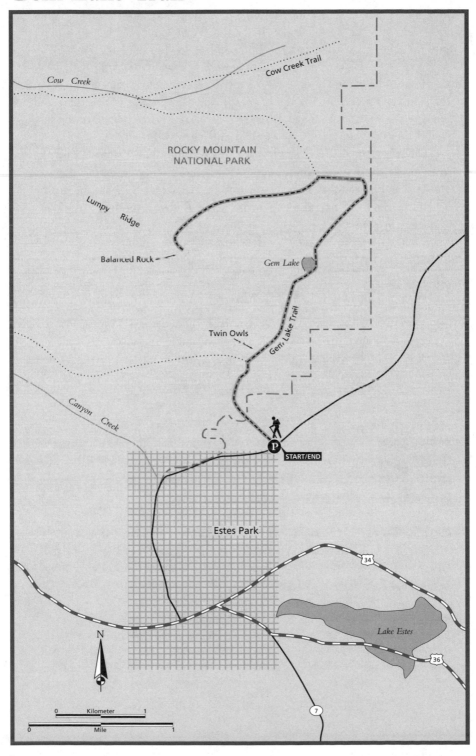

Cow Creek Trail

Cow Creek

ROCKY MOUNTAIN
NATIONAL PARK

Lumpy Ridge

Balanced Rock

Gem Lake

Twin Owls

Gen Lake Trail

Canyon Creek

P START/END

Estes Park

34

Lake Estes

36

7

N

| 0 | Kilometer | 1 |
| 0 | Mile | 1 |

looking for a good, hard workout. At 0.8 mile the trail enters a small gulch and intersects with the Devils Gulch Trail on the left. Continue straight and up into the pines up a steep, rocky section and overlook to the left. Take a break and take in the views. The trail climbs a series of switchbacks through small granite formations and levels out for a moment, revealing spectacular views to the south and west. This is another great place to sit on the granite rocks and enjoy views. At the 1.2-mile mark the trail drops down into a small ravine surrounded by tall granite cliffs. The trail is quite narrow through this section and crosses over a small stream surrounded by quaking aspens. Wild raspberries grow profusely along the trail in the late summer months and are quite tasty when ripe. The trail begins a steep climb up several switchbacks; be on the lookout to the left for a weird rock formation with a hole through the middle. Continue up past a solar-powered outhouse to a ridgeline. A short scramble leads to the tiny lake nestled quaintly below the short, granite walls. Relax for a moment and retrace your route back to the trailhead.

Option: Instead of retracing your route back to the trailhead, you can extend your hike and travel for another 1.8 miles to the precipitous Balanced Rock. Skirt the lake on the left, scramble through a passage in the rock walls, and descend toward Cow Creek. At 0.9 mile past the lake you take a left turn and follow the trail for 0.9 mile to the rock. Return as you came.

Glacier Gorge

Highlights: *In my opinion this is the most beautiful spot in Rocky Mountain National Park. Spectacular scenery, beautiful wildflowers, cascading waterfalls, and beautiful alpine lakes are what you will find on your hike into Glacier Gorge. Bring along a fishing rod and a camera.*

Season: June to October.
Distance: 4.8 miles one way.
Difficulty: Moderate to strenuous.
Maps: Trails Illustrated Rocky Mountain National Park #200.

Management: Rocky Mountain National Park/USDA Forest Service.
Trail conditions: Well-traveled and smooth going on the first mile of the trail. The trail becomes quite rocky up to Black Lake.

Glacier Gorge

To Estes Park, 36

Bear Lake Road

Bear Lake ℗

℗

START/END

Glacier Creek

Alberta Falls

North Longs Peak Trail

Glacier Falls

Loch Vale

Mills Lake

Glacier

Jewel Lake

Glacier Gorge Campsite

Taylor Peak
13,152 ft.

Thatchtop
12,668 ft.

Gorge

Ribbon Falls

Blue Lake

Black Lake

Powell Peak
13,208 ft.

McHenrys Peak
13,327 ft.

N

0   Kilometer   2
0   Mile   2

Finding the trailhead: From Estes Park head west on U.S. Highway 36 past the Rocky Mountain National Park entrance station. Travel 0.3 mile past the ranger station and go left on Bear Lake Road for 8.5 miles to a parking area at a sharp hairpin turn. The hike starts here.

Key points:
0.6 Alberta Falls.
1.9 Trail to Loch Vale.
2.5 Mills Lake.
3.5 Glacier Gorge Campsite.
4.8 Black Lake.

The hike: Cross the road and reach the trailhead. Go left, following the sign for Alberta Falls. Cross a bridge and ignore a trail on the right. Continue straight and enjoy easy hiking through a forest of aspens, spruce, and lodgepole pines. Cross over several bridges and climb to Alberta Falls. Step to the left and enjoy the spectacular waterfall that has cut an impressive gorge with its forceful waters. Alberta Falls is a mere 0.6 mile from the trailhead and can be extremely crowded. Don't worry, like most trails in the park, the farther away from the trailhead you get, the fewer people there are. After the falls the trail begins a steady climb up several long switchbacks. Towering granite cliffs are off to the right and the views open up to the north, east, and west. At around the 1.4-mile mark you reach a junction with the North Longs Peak Trail on the left. Continue straight. Reach a high point and then follow the trail down a gentle grade through a scree slope, with Glacier Creek on the left. The tops of the towering rock walls of Spearhead and Chiefhead Peaks can be seen in a commanding position at the western end of Glacier Gorge. Drop down through the pines and reach a trail junction. The trail to Loch Vale goes to the right. You continue straight and down, crossing Icy Brook and then a log bridge over Glacier Creek. The trail goes right and follows granite steps up to where the trail seems to disappear. Don't panic. Follow cairns up through granite slick

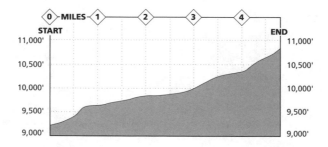

rock to Mills Lake and spectacular views of Glacier Gorge. Take a break on one of the many rocks near the shoreline of this spectacular, alpine lake. Mills Lake is extremely popular with anglers and for some hikers is a destination in itself. The trail now goes a little left into the pines and avoids the moist areas around the shoreline of Mills Lake. Travel through the pines and reach Jewel Lake. Jewel Lake sits in an open area surrounded by thick bog grasses and alpine wildflowers. The trail stays left of the lake and travels across several wood boardwalks through the moist area around the lake. Enjoy the wildflowers that grow profusely in the rich, fertile soil. After crossing the boardwalks the trail stays close to Glacier Creek; use boulders to avoid getting your feet wet. Wildflowers bloom everywhere and light up the trail with their brilliant colors. At around the 3.5-mile mark arrive at a trail junction at a bridge. The Glacier Gorge Campsite lies to the right over the stream. You continue straight and up using stone stairs to negotiate a steep section past a small waterfall. The trail goes left up a talus slope away from the stream, following rock cairns up to a level area near Black Lake. Skirt the lake on the left, using a rock shelf to access the trail on the other side. Climb up and down and reach a beautiful open area near the west end of Black Lake. This cirque is absolutely beautiful and can't be described with my meager writing skills. Ribbon Falls lies up and to the right as do the towering, rocky summits of Arrowhead and McHenrys Peaks. Straight ahead lie the impressive vertical rock summits of Spearhead and Chiefhead Peaks, dominating the western skyline. Hopefully you brought a camera, and if you brought a lunch, this is the spot to eat it. A climber's trail goes up to the left along a creek and gains a flat area filled with small tarns and bogs. Feel free to explore if you have the time or energy. This hike ends at Black Lake. Retrace your route back to the trailhead.

Camping: At group campsites. A permit is required.

8

Estes Cone

Highlights: *Incredible views, an abandoned mine, and beautiful hiking on a well-maintained trail are the main attractions on this great hike up to the symmetrical summit of Estes Cone. One of the best short hikes in Rocky Mountain National Park.*

Season: May to November.
Distance: 3.2 miles one way.
Difficulty: Moderate to strenuous. The last grunt up to the summit is quite steep and strenuous.
Maps: Trails Illustrated Rocky Mountain National Park #200.

Management: Rocky Mountain National Park/USDA Forest Service.
Trail conditions: Well-traveled and smooth going on the first mile of the trail. The upper section is rocky and the trail all but disappears near the rocky summit of Estes Cone.

Finding the trailhead: From Boulder take U.S. Highway 36 to the town of Lyons. Turn left on Colorado Highway 7 and travel 22 miles. Turn left at a sign for the Longs Peak Trailhead. Go 1 mile to the Longs Peak Trailhead, campground, ranger station, and parking area.

Key points:
0.5 The trail forks.
1.4 Eugenia Mine site and Inn Brook.
1.8 Moore Park Campsite.
2.0 Trail junction.
2.5 Storm Pass.
3.2 Estes Cone.

The hike: This hike starts at the very popular Longs Peak Trailhead. The trailhead is extremely busy during the summer months, and it is difficult to secure a parking spot during this time. Arrive early or do the hike during the

Estes Cone

Estes Cone 11,006 ft.

Storm Pass 10,321 ft.

Eugenia Mine

Moore Park

Pine Ridge

Storm Pass Trail

Inn Brook

To Estes Park

Longs Peak Campground

START/END

Goblins Forest Campground

Alpine Brook

Battle Mountain Group Campsite

Battle Mountain Trail

Battle Mountain 12,044 ft.

Longs Peak Trail

Peacock Pool

Mt. Lady Washington 13,281 ft.

Chasm Lake

Longs Peak 14,255 ft.

Mt. Meeker 13,911 ft.

To Lyons

7

N

Kilometer

Mile

week to increase your chances of getting a parking spot. The start of the hike follows the Longs Peak Trail up through a dense coniferous forest on a well-maintained trail. The trail climbs to a junction with the Storm Pass Trail. At around the 0.5-mile mark and at the trail junction, the Estes Cone comes into view. Go right at the trail junction, following the trail into a mixed forest of aspens and pines. The trail climbs, descends, and traverses below Pine Ridge; at the 1.4-mile mark the trail crosses over Inn Brook via a wood footbridge to the Eugenia Mine site. All that is left of the old mine are an old, rusted boiler, tailings, and logs from the Norwall cabin. Carl P. Norwall worked the mine in the early 1900s but soon left the area because all his work proved to be fruitless. Skirt the cabin on the right and drop down through a dense forest of lodgepole pines to a small, open meadow. The meadow is quite lush, and during the summer months wildflowers grow profusely in this open area. At around the 1.8-mile mark are a number of campsites. The Moore Park Campsite is in a pleasing setting along the edge of the meadow and offers a beautiful place to stop and spend the night. Past the campsite you arrive at the 2.0-mile mark and a trail junction. Going right takes you to private property. Make a sharp left and begin climbing up a steep, forested slope to Storm Pass. The trail climbs steeply between rocks and wooden log stairs, with stunning views of the east face of Longs Peak on the left and the Estes Cone straight ahead. At 2.5 miles you reach the pass. Storm Pass is marked with trail signs and a large rock cairn. Take a short break here before the final grunt to the summit. The Storm Pass Cutoff Trail on the right is a new trail (in 2001) that goes right and down to the Lily Lake Trailhead. Follow the Estes Cone Trail up through the limber pines, with the Estes Cone summit looming straight ahead. Enjoy the views, which become more spectacular the higher you climb. Once out of the trees the trail climbs up through the rocks, following small rock cairns that guide you through the rock walls. Reach a small flat area, then head up and right to the true summit of the Estes Cone. Relax on the summit and enjoy spectacular views in all directions. Retrace your route back to the trailhead.

Camping: At the trailhead and at Moore Park.

9 Chasm Lake

Highlights: *Chasm Lake lies nestled in a rocky alpine cirque below the towering summits of Longs Peak (14,255 feet) and Mount Meeker (13,911 feet), the two highest summits in Rocky Mountain National Park. The cirque is absolutely stunning and is one of the most beautiful spots in all of Colorado. Do this hike!*

Season: June to October.
Distance: 4.2 miles one way.
Difficulty: Moderate to strenuous.
Maps: Trails Illustrated Rocky Mountain National Park #200.
Management: Rocky Mountain National Park/USDA Forest Service.

Trail conditions: Well-traveled and smooth going on the first mile of the trail. The trail becomes quite rocky the closer you get to the lake.

Finding the trailhead: From Boulder take U.S. Highway 36 to the town of Lyons. Turn left on Colorado Highway 7 and travel 22 miles. Turn left at a sign for the Longs Peak Trailhead. Go 1 mile to the Longs Peak Trailhead, campground, ranger station, and parking area.

Key points:
0.5 The trail forks.
1.3 Goblins Forest Campground.
2.5 Battle Mountain Group Campsite.
3.8 Chasm Lake junction.
4.2 Chasm Lake.

The hike: This hike starts at the very popular Longs Peak Trailhead. The trailhead is extremely busy during the summer months, and it is difficult to secure a parking spot during this time. Having hiked this trail at least fifteen times for climbing trips to the east face of Longs Peak, I recommend that you arrive early or do the hike during the week to increase your chances of getting a parking spot. The hike follows the Longs Peak Trail up through a dense coniferous forest on a well-maintained trail. It then climbs up to the junction with the Storm Pass Trail. At the trail junction continue straight on the Longs Peak Trail and travel across Pine Ridge up to Alpine Brook. At around the 1.0-mile mark Alpine Brook can be seen and heard on the left of the trail. Switchback up, with views to the east of the double peaks, aptly named Twin Sisters. At around the 1.3-mile mark you pass the Goblins Forest Campground on the left. The sheer rock wall of the east face of Longs Peak comes into view

Chasm Lake

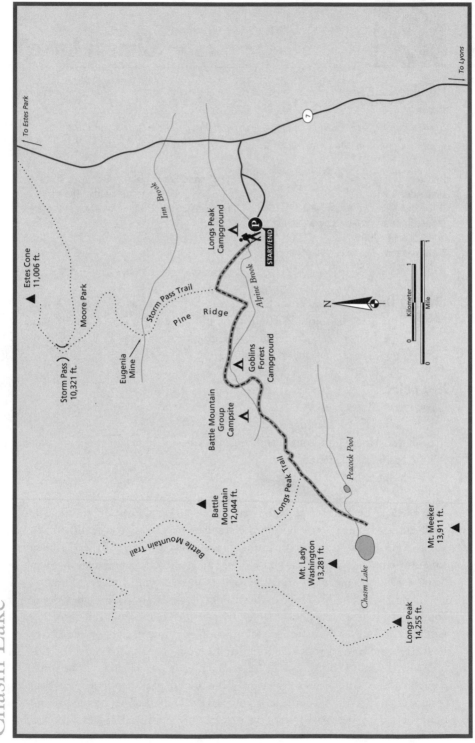

To Estes Park

To Lyons

7

Estes Cone
11,006 ft.

Moore Park

Storm Pass
10,321 ft.

Inn Brook

Storm Pass Trail

Eugenia
Mine

Pine Ridge

Longs Peak
Campground

Alpine Brook

START/END

P

Goblins Forest
Campground

Battle Mountain
Group Campsite

Battle Mountain Trail

Battle
Mountain
12,044 ft.

Longs Peak Trail

Peacock Pool

Mt. Lady
Washington
13,281 ft.

Mt. Meeker
13,911 ft.

Chasm Lake

Longs Peak
14,255 ft.

N

Kilometer   1
0

Mile   1
0

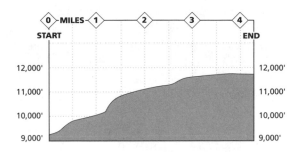

for the first time. It is quite impressive! The trail stays to the right of Alpine Brook and travels through a small scree garden up to Larkspur Creek. Things start to get serious from here on. Cross over Larkspur Creek and begin a steep climb up several switchbacks to Alpine Brook. At Alpine Brook take a break and look around at the beautiful alpine flowers that grow in the moist soil around the banks of the creek. What a beautiful spot! Time to move on. The trail now travels into Mill Moraine and up to timberline. Stunted flag trees dot the landscape and seem to be hanging on for dear life. The harsh conditions at this altitude make normal growth all but impossible for these hardy trees with branches on one side. Continue climbing steeply into patches of rugged alpine grasses and be on the lookout for tiny, alpine flowers that somehow manage to blossom in harsh conditions. Most people start to feel the effects of the altitude at this point. Drink lots of water and pace yourself. Krummholz trees begin to appear as you approach Battle Mountain Group Campsite on the right of the trail and across Alpine Brook. These low-lying trees cling to the ground to survive in what is almost winter-like weather year-round. The trees almost look like ground cover but in spite of their appearance can live to be hundreds of years old. The trail keeps climbing, and if you want to reach Chasm Lake, so do you. Keep moving; before you know it you reach a trail junction and a breathtaking view

Longs Peak

of the east face of Longs Peak. The trail to the right continues up into the boulder field and to the summit of Longs Peak. You continue straight and along the southern flank of Mount Lady Washington (13,281 feet). The trail

45

climbs briefly, then makes a gradual descent to Chasm Lake. Off to the left are Peacock Pool and Columbine Falls. Reach Chasm Meadows and enjoy the abundant wildflowers. Cross a small stream and travel past the ranger's rescue cabin. Climb up through the rocks and voila; arrive at beautiful Chasm Lake.

Camping: At the trailhead and at group campsites. A permit is required.

10

Calypso Cascades

Highlights: *A great hike down into the Wild Basin area of Rocky Mountain National Park and Calypso Cascades. Calypso Cascades is a beautiful, tumbling waterfall that drops more than 100 feet through a forested hillside formed by the raging waters of North St. Vrain Creek. The trails in Rocky Mountain National Park are well maintained and marked with accurate distances at most trail junctions.*

Season: June to October.
Distance: 3.1 miles one way.
Difficulty: Moderate.
Maps: Trails Illustrated Rocky Mountain National Park #200.
Management: Rocky Mountain National Park/USDA Forest Service.

Trail conditions: Well-traveled and smooth going on the first mile of the trail. The trail becomes rocky and root-filled near Calypso Cascades.

Finding the trailhead: From Boulder take U.S. Highway 36 to the town of Lyons. Turn left on Colorado Highway 7 and travel 17 miles to Allenspark. Turn left into Allenspark and make a right on County Road 90 (at the post office). Travel 1.2 miles to a fork in the road. Bear left at the fork and travel 1.0 mile to the Allenspark Trailhead on the left. Park here to start the hike.

Calypso Cascades

To Estes Park

Longs Peak
14,255 ft.

Mt. Meeker
13,911 ft.

Wild Basin
Ranger Station

7

7

To Nederland

Allenspark

START/END

Allenspark Trail

North St. Vrain Creek

Finch Lake Trail

Ouzel Falls

Calypso Cascades

Finch Lake

Blue Bird Lake Trail

Cony Creek

Pear Lake

Copeland Mountain
13,176 ft.

St. Vrain Mountain
12,162 ft.

N

Kilometer

Mile

Key points:
0.5 Small stream crossing.
0.8 Trail junction.
1.8 Trail to Calypso Cascades and Ouzel Falls.
3.1 Calypso Cascades.

The hike: From the trailhead the trail makes a gentle climb through dense spruce forest to a small stream crossing. The trail up to this point is fairly smooth and free of rocks. Beyond the creek the trail climbs to a trail junction on rockier tread, still deep in the trees, with limited views to the north. At the trail junction you go left, following the sign to Finch Lake. The trail becomes extremely rocky and climbs a stair of stone, with good views of Mount Meeker and Longs Peak. At the 1.8-mile mark you arrive at a three-way trail junction. Going right takes you to the Wild Basin Ranger Station, going left leads to Finch Lake, and straight ahead is your route to Calypso Cascades. The trail drops at a nice grade, with spruce trees and wildflowers hugging the trail. There are excellent views to the west, with Copeland Mountain (13,176 feet) dominating the skyline on the eastern side of the Continental Divide. To the north you can catch a glimpse of Mount Meeker (13,911 feet) and Longs Peak (14,255 feet), the highest point in Rocky Mountain National Park.

Remains of the 1978 Ouzel Fire are evident in this area as many burned trees cover the steep slopes along the trail. The fire consumed more than a thousand acres of prime forested land and almost took out the town of Allenspark before firefighters controlled the spreading flames. The fire also made the National Park Service review it's policies on let-burn fires. Much regeneration has taken place since the fire, and the landscape is slowly returning to what it was before the mishap.

Continue down over a wood bridge across a drainage. The sound of the falls can be heard in the distance and becomes louder with every step you take down the trail. Be on the lookout for wildflowers along this section of the trail. Paintbrushes, columbines, and other colorful flowers line the hillsides, giving life to what just twenty-four years ago was a charred, barren landscape. The trail becomes rocky as you near the falls and switchbacks down to two bridges that span the creek at a trail junction. The bridges are a great spot from which to view the falls and take pictures. The falls are named for the fairy slipper orchid (Calypso bulbosa), a rare flower that blooms along the falls and trail during late spring and early summer. This area can be extremely crowded on the weekends during the summer months. If you want to extend your hike, follow the signs for Ouzel Falls, which is just under a mile away. After enjoying the falls retrace your route back to the Allenspark Trailhead.

11

Finch Lake

Highlights: *This is a great one- or two-day hike in the Wild Basin area of Rocky Mountain National Park. Wildflowers, great views, and a beautiful alpine lake are the rewards for your efforts in this southern section of Rocky Mountain National Park.*

Season: June to October.
Distance: 4.1 miles one way.
Difficulty: Moderate.
Maps: Trails Illustrated Rocky Mountain National Park #200.

Management: Rocky Mountain National Park/USDA Forest Service.
Trail conditions: Well-traveled and smooth going on the first mile of the trail. After that expect very rocky and root-filled tread all the way to Finch Lake.

Finding the trailhead: From Boulder take U.S. Highway 36 to the town of Lyons. Turn left on Colorado Highway 7 and travel 17 miles to Allenspark. Turn left into Allenspark and make a right on County Road 90 (at the post office). Travel 1.2 miles to a fork in the road. Bear left at the fork and travel 1.0 mile to the Allenspark Trailhead on the left. Park here to start the hike.

Key points:
0.5 Small stream crossing.
0.8 Trail junction.
1.8 Trail to Ouzel Falls.
2.2 Remnants of the Ouzel Fire.
3.5 Small bridge over North St. Vrain Creek.
4.1 Finch Lake.

The hike: From the trailhead the trail makes a gentle climb through dense spruce forest to a small stream crossing. The trail up to this point is fairly smooth and free of rocks. Beyond the creek the trail climbs to a trail junction on rockier tread, still deep in the trees, with limited views to the north. At the trail junction you go left, following the sign to Finch Lake. The trail becomes extremely rocky and climbs a stair of stone, with good views of Mount Meeker (13,911 feet) and Longs Peak (14,255 feet). At the 1.8-mile mark you arrive at a trail junction. Going right takes you to the Wild Basin Ranger Station; straight ahead and a little over a mile away is Ouzel Falls. For this hike you go up and left, following the Finch Lake Trail. The trail climbs at a gentle grade

Finch Lake

To Estes Park

Longs Peak
14,255 ft.

Mt. Meeker
13,911 ft.

Wild Basin
Ranger Station

7

7

To Nederland

N

Allenspark

START/END

P

Allenspark
Trail

Finch Lake Trail

North St. Vrain Creek

Calypso
Cascades

Ouzel Falls

Blue Bird Lake Trail

Copeland
Mountain
13,176 ft.

Pear Lake

Cony Creek

Finch Lake

St. Vrain Mountain
12,162 ft.

Kilometer

Mile

0   2

0   2

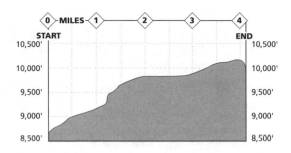

into the remnants of 1978 Ouzel Fire. The fire consumed more than a thousand acres of timber and left a huge black scar on the surrounding landscape. The trail cuts right through a large stand of charred trees and is quite spooky looking. Looking around you will notice how the forest has begun to rejuvenate itself, with batches of blueberry bushes, small stands of aspen and pine trees, and beautiful wildflowers growing. The most common flowers along this section of the trail are the narrowleaf puccoon, alpine daisy, and my favorite wildflower, the elephantella. There are great views through the dead trees to the north and west, with snow-covered peaks dotting the skyline. The rocky trail stays fairly level as you work your way through a forest of moss-draped pines to a small bridge over North St. Vrain Creek. The day I hiked the trail a group of trail-builders were working on removing rocks, trees, and other debris. They were also making small bridges over the wet areas, making travel through this section much easier. Hats off to these folks for all their hard work. Once past the bridge the trail drops down steeply on very rocky tread to your destination, Finch Lake. A sign will point you to campsites if you are staying overnight. The lake is stocked with cutthroat trout, so bring a fishing rod and enjoy an afternoon of great fishing in a beautiful setting. If you plan on spending the night, a written permit from Rocky Mountain National Park is required. For the return trip, retrace your route back to the trailhead.

Camping: At Finch Lake.

12

Lion Gulch Trail

Highlights: *A beautiful hike up through Lion Gulch to Homestead Meadow, the site of numerous, abandoned settlements from the late 1800s and early 1900s.*

Season: Early spring to late autumn.
Distance: 2.8 miles one way.
Difficulty: Moderate to strenuous.
Maps: Trails Illustrated Cache la Poudre–Big Thompson #101.

Management: Roosevelt National Forest.
Trail conditions: The trail is extremely root-filled and rocky in certain sections.

Finding the trailhead: From Boulder follow U.S. Highway 36 to the town of Lyons. Travel through Lyons and then 12.2 miles on US 36 toward Estes Park to the Lion Gulch Trailhead on the left.

Key points:
0.3 First footbridge.
0.5 Second footbridge.
0.9 Third footbridge.
2.0 Last of the stream crossings.
2.7 Homestead Meadow.
2.8 Walker Homestead.

The hike: From the parking area, pass the restroom on the right and go down to the first footbridge. Cross over the bridge and travel through a small meadow into the trees and up to the second footbridge. Cross the footbridge; on the other side the trail forks. Right is for horses and left is for hikers. Go left up the steep, rocky hill on rock and wood steps. The trail climbs away from the creek on extremely rocky tread. Gain the ridge, with US 36 on the right. Drop again to the creek and through a small open meadow filled with pine and

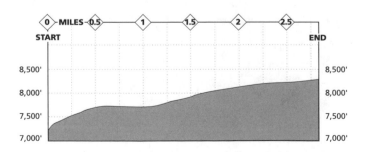

Lion Gulch Trail

To Estes Park

To Lyons

START/END

P

Creek crossings

Creek crossings

Lion Gulch Trail 949

Homestead

Walke Homestead

Information kiosk

Homestead

Homestead Meadow

Homestead

Homestead

Pierson Park Trail 1000

N

Kilometer

Mile

0 1

0 1

young aspen trees. Cross over the third footbridge and begin a short climb. The trail now travels through a dense forest of beautiful ponderosa pines, Douglas firs, and mature aspen trees. At one point the moss-covered trees create a canopy and the trail is cushioned with fragrant needles. Make several stream crossings via log bridges, and at around the 1.7-mile mark begin a steep, narrow climb away from the creek. This trail is very popular with horseback riders. If you happen to meet riders, give the right of way and do not spook the horses. Certain sections of the trail are quite narrow, and spooking the horses could result in injury to horse and rider. At around the 2.0-mile mark you cross the creek for the last time, with a small waterfall beside the trail. Continue climbing on the narrow trail, with granite rock formations on the right and numerous downed trees on the left. The trees must have fallen victim to some disease or beetle infestation. The rugged country surrounding the trail is the perfect environment for mountain lions, and several of the big cats have been seen in the area. At around the 2.3-mile mark the trail follows what seems to be an old wagon road, and Homestead Meadow appears. Tall meadow grasses, wildflowers, and proud ponderosas surround the trail up to a kiosk. Be on the lookout for elk that graze on the meadow grasses. At around the 2.6-mile mark arrive at the kiosk, which has information on the early settlers of the area. Read the information and continue up the trail past a water trough to a trail junction. At the 2.7-mile mark several trail markers give mileage to various homesteads. For this hike continue straight up the open meadow to the Walker Homestead on the right at the 2.8-mile mark. Feel free to explore the many miles of trails and the various homesteads in the area, or take a break and enjoy some lunch before heading back to the Lion Gulch Trailhead.

Camping: Along the trail and at Homestead Meadow.

13

Button Rock Preserve

Highlights: *Fishing, wildlife viewing, and exceptional hiking can be found in the Button Rock Preserve, and this hike will allow you the opportunity to experience all of these activities.*

Season: Early spring to late autumn.
Distance: 5.9-mile loop.
Difficulty: Moderate.
Maps: Boulder County, USGS, and City of Longmont/Button Rock Preserve.

Management: City of Longmont.
Trail conditions: The lower section follows a smooth service road and the upper section of the hike travels through a short, rocky section.

Finding the trailhead: From the town of Lyons follow U.S. Highway 36 toward Estes Park for 3.8 miles to County Road 80. Go left on CR 80 and travels 2.8 miles to a parking area and the start of the hike.

Key points:
1.2 Sleepy Lion Trail junction.
2.9 Junction with the Hall Ranch Trail.
3.5 Ralph Price Reservoir.
5.9 Back at the trailhead.

Button Rock Preserve

Button Rock Preserve

To Lyons, 36
County Road 80
North St. Vrain Creek
START/END
P
Longmont Reservoir
Antelope Park
Deadman Gulch
Sleepy Lion Trail
Ralph Price Reservoir
Long Gulch
To Hall Ranch Open Space

N

Kilometer
0   1
Mile
0

The hike: From the parking area follow the road up past a gate. Pass a handicap-accessed trail on the left and begin a gradual climb up the road, passing Longmont Reservoir on the right. Several rock walls on the right at the spillway are popular with rock climbers, and during the summer months you might see them clawing their way up the granite walls. Continue up the service road, with the North St. Vrain Creek on the right, to the Sleepy Lion Trail on the left. This area is popular for fly-fishing and can be quite crowded during the summer months. At around the 1.2-mile mark go left on the Sleepy Lion Trail into the trees and up Deadman Gulch. The trail now begins a steep climb on a smooth, narrow trail to a beautiful meadow through thick stands of ponderosa pines and Douglas firs. The trail winds back to the north, is easy to follow, and is quite pleasant, with views to the north. At around the 2.0 mile mark the trail leaves the forest and cuts across a beautiful, open meadow with great views of Rocky Mountain National Park. The meadow is quite picturesque, with wildflowers and yuccas growing along with tall meadow grasses. This is a good spot to take a break. After traveling through the meadow the trail heads back into the trees and drops down into the ponderosa and pine trees. The elevation loss doesn't last long, and the trail begins to climb through and around several boulders and follows an old fence line. Before long you reach a junction with a new trail that links Hall Ranch Open Space with the Sleepy Lion Trail. Continue on the Sleepy Lion Trail, with views to the north and the Ralph Price Reservoir. Skirt past several large boulders, with open views to the north, and reach an old service road. Go right on the road and begin the descent to the spillway. The road switchbacks down through the pines and just before the spillway cuts through a narrow gulch filled with willows, aspens, and pines. Reach the service road and contour around the spillway, with it's water shooting out forcefully into North St. Vrain Creek. Follow the road down past a restroom and along the creek back to the parking area and the end of the hike.

The area you just traveled through is a wildlife preserve and is open to foot travel only. The City of Longmont built the Ralph Price Reservoir in the late 1960s; it is named for a former mayor. In the winter fishing is not allowed at the reservoir and at other times is by permit only. Bald eagles roost and hunt along the shores of the reservoir, and bighorn sheep can be seen in the more remote areas above and around the dam.

14 Hall Ranch

Highlights: *One of the best day hikes in the Estes Park/Lyons area. Beautiful vistas, stunning sandstone cliffs, abundant wildlife, cacti, and flower-filled meadows are what you are going to see on this hike. Pick up a Hall Ranch brochure from the kiosk and enhance your hike by reading the information in the brochure.*

Season: Year-round.
Distance: 10.0-mile loop.
Difficulty: Moderate.
Maps: Boulder County Open Space/Hall Ranch.

Management: Boulder County Open Space.
Trail conditions: The trail ranges from very smooth to extremely rocky.

Finding the trailhead: From Boulder travel west on U.S. Highway 36 to Lyons and a junction with Colorado Highway 7. Go left on CO 7 for 1.3 miles to the Hall Ranch Open Space trailhead and parking on the right.

Key Points:
0.8 Old service road.
2.1 Top of the hill and bench.
3.8 Start of the Nelson Loop.
4.0 Bridge.
4.4 Old homestead.
6.2 Back at the Bitterbrush Trail.
10.0 Back at the parking area/trailhead.

The hike: From the upper parking area travel past the kiosk and restrooms. Access the Bitterbrush Trail and the start of the hike. Follow the well-marked Bitterbrush Trail west. Looking north you'll see impressive sandstone bluffs overlooking the trail, evidence of the constant change the Earth undergoes. These exposed cliffs are at the start of where the Rocky Mountains meet the flat, open plains, and the cliffs you are admiring now are the result of changes in the Earth almost 1.5 billion years ago.

Hall Ranch

To Estes Park

Lyons

36

7

START/END

Bitterbrush Trail

Nighthawk Trail

South St. Vrain Creek

Nelson Homestead

Nelson Loop

To Allenspark

N

Kilometer

Mile

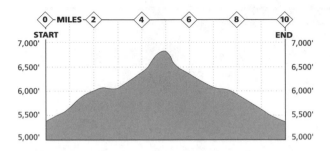

The trail curves around on the north side of a hill through an area of granite boulders, cacti, mahogany oak, and tall prairie grasses. Reach a service road at around the 0.8-mile mark and drop into a narrow gulch. Past a rocky section the trail starts to climb to the north. Yuccas, cacti, and ponderosas line the trail as you start to gain altitude. Climb past several rocky sections (look on the ground for quartz crystals) and switchback up to a level area at the 2.1-mile mark. Take a break on the bench and admire panoramic views to the south, west, and east. Continue north past an interpretive sign, with a large black-tailed prairie dog colony in a large open meadow on the left. The trail makes a short drop and hugs the north side of the meadow, making a big sweep back to the west. Look for deer and other wildlife that calls this beautiful place home in the open meadow and tall grasses. At around the 2.8-mile mark pass a second interpretive sign and follow the trail into a beautiful stand of young ponderosa trees. Looming Mount Meeker (13,911 feet) and Longs Peak (14,255 feet) fill the western skyline. At around the 3.4-mile mark look to the right and down into a rock-filled gully. Several large cliffs teeter on the hillside and are quite an impressive sight. At the 3.8-mile mark you arrive at a trail junction. Time to make a decision: do the Nelson Loop or turn back.

Let's do the Nelson Loop. Turn left and travel into an open meadow, with great views to the south. Reach a bridge at the 4.0-mile mark and switchback up through the ponderosas to a beautiful, wide-open meadow. Take in the views to the west and travel down to old Nelson Homestead on the right. Past the homestead the trail meets with the Nighthawk Trail on the left at the 4.9-mile mark. The Nighthawk Trail is 4.1 miles long and meets with the Sleepy Lion Trail at Button Rock Preserve (see hike #13). The trail curves around the open meadow and heads back to the north. Reach a nice stand of ponderosas and follow the twisting trail back to the start of the Nelson Loop and Bitterbrush Trail. From this point retrace your route back down the Bitterbrush Trail to the parking area and the trailhead. This is a popular trail with mountain cyclists and equestrians. It is a multi-use trail so show common courtesy to all trail users.

15

Rabbit Mountain

Highlights: *A fantastic hike with expansive views of the northern foothills; east to the plains; and west to the Indians Peaks, Rocky Mountain National Park, and the Continental Divide. This hike takes you through stands of ponderosas and open meadows filled with cacti, yuccas, and wildflowers. Wildlife is abundant and can be seen year-round.*

Season: Year-round.
Distance: 4.1-mile loop.
Difficulty: Moderate.
Maps: Boulder County Open Space/Rabbit Mountain.

Management: Boulder County Open Space.
Trail conditions: Rocky.

Finding the trailhead: From Boulder follow U.S. Highway 36 north to the town of Lyons. Turn east on Colorado Highway 66 and travel 3.0 miles to North 53d Street. Turn left on North 53d Street and travel 3.0 miles to the trailhead and parking area.

Key Points:
0.5 Junction with the Little Thompson Overlook Trail.
0.9 Bench.
1.0 Eagle Wind Trail splits.
3.1 End of the loop.
3.5 Go left back to the parking area.
4.1 Back at the trailhead.

The hike: From the parking area reach the kiosk, grab a brochure, and take the Eagle Wind Trail east. The trail cuts across a hill on two switchbacks, travels through a recent burn area, and climbs to a junction with the Little Thompson Overlook Trail at the 0.5-mile mark. Go right at the trail junction across the service road and head south. There are great views of the Flatirons to the south and Mount Meeker (13,911 feet) and Longs Peak (14,255 feet) to the west. At around the 0.9-mile mark you reach a bench on the left side of the trail, facing west. This is a good spot to take a break and enjoy expansive views to the west and the Continental Divide. The trail continues south through an area of thick mahogany oak, prickly pear cacti, and tall prairie grasses to where the trail splits. Go right and soon enter into a stand of beautiful ponderosa pines. Lichen-covered rocks are scattered on and around the trail along with

Rabbit Mountain

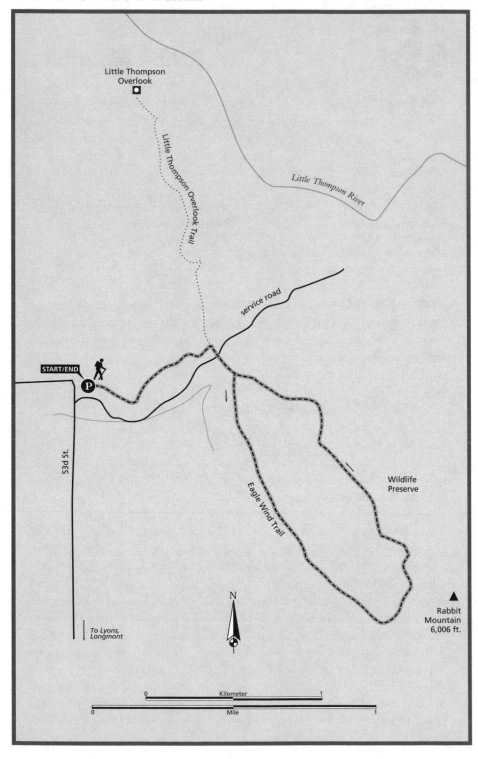

Little Thompson
Overlook

Little Thompson River

Little Thompson Overlook Trail

service road

START/END

53d St.

Wildlife
Preserve

Eagle Wind Trail

To Lyons,
Longmont

Rabbit
Mountain
6,006 ft.

N

| 0 | Kilometer | 1 |
| 0 | Mile | 1 |

yuccas and small cacti. At around the 1.5-mile mark the trail cuts through a small open meadow and heads to the east. Rattlesnakes are common around Rabbit Mountain and like to warm themselves on sunny slopes and boulders. Use caution from mid-March to mid-October when hiking around Rabbit Mountain. The trail makes a slight drop, then climbs a short hill back to the north, passing a wildlife-sensitive area on the right. There is no public access to the right of the trail, so respect the rules and obey the posted signs. The views to the north are beautiful and reveal sharp-cut ridges and steep-sloped hills. The trail reaches an old road at the 2.5-mile mark, and the hike follows the rocky road down and to the right through the ponderosas. At around the 2.9-mile mark the trail bears to the right and in 0.2 mile you arrive back at a familiar trail junction and the end of the loop. From this point retrace your route back to the trailhead.

Rabbit Mountain is a wonderful place to view wildlife. The abundance of prairie grasses and mahogany shrubs makes this area an important winter feeding area for both white-tailed and mule deer. In a rugged, rocky area like Rabbit Mountain and with large herds of deer, more than likely you will find mountain lions, and it is no surprise that they have been spotted at Rabbit Mountain. The tall grasses and low-lying shrubs also provide a feeding area and home to small rodents. In turn the rodents attract high-flying raptors. There are also rattlesnakes, which are not aggressive, will not run you down, and for the most part want to be left alone. If you happen to see one of these beautiful reptiles, give the snake a lot of room and more than likely it will avoid you.

Boulder,
Foothills and
MOUNTAINS

16 Ceran St. Vrain Trail

Highlights: *A beautiful trail through lodgepole pines along South St. Vrain Creek. Excellent family hike with good campsites, fishing, and access. Great spot for early summer wildflowers.*

Season: Early spring to late autumn.
Distance: 3.1 miles one way.
Difficulty: Strenuous.
Maps: Trails Illustrated Indian Peaks/Gold Hill #102.

Management: Boulder Ranger District, USDA Forest Service.
Trail conditions: The trail is smooth along the creek and rocky near Miller Rocks.

Finding the trailhead: From Broadway and Canyon in Boulder, go north on Broadway for 4.0 miles to Lee Hill Road. Turn left and follow Lee Hill Road to Old Stage Road; follow Old Stage Road for 4.0 miles to Lefthand Canyon Road. Turn left on Lefthand Canyon to Jamestown. Travel 4.7 miles past Jamestown to the turnoff for the trailhead. Go right into the parking area and trailhead.

Key points:

1.9 Go left and up.
2.1 Trail junction at top of the hill. Go left and up.
2.4 Trail junction. Go right.
2.7 Go left.
3.1 Miller Rocks on the right.

The hike: The trailhead starts at a bridge over South St. Vrain Creek and guides you into a beautiful forest of lodgepole pines and wildflowers. This section of the trail is popular with campers and anglers and can be very crowded on weekends during the summer months. The area near the trailhead and the smooth water-worn rocks in the river is an excellent spot to just hang out, eat some lunch, and enjoy the tumbling waters. The trail climbs a short distance, then becomes narrow, with steep dropoffs to the right. Be on the lookout for wildflowers and clusters of beautiful fairy slipper orchids during the early summer months. (The fairy slipper is a rare flower of the orchid family that grows in the moist, shady evergreen forest of the Rocky Mountain foothills, montane, and subalpine ecosystems from Alaska in the north to New Mexico in the south.) The trail pulls away from the river and makes a healthy descent to a trail junction at the 1.9-mile mark. Go left and up away from the river to a trail junc-

Ceran St. Vrain Trail

tion at the top of the hill. Go left again, up to another trail junction. The hike goes right on a narrow trail up to a junction with an old logging road. Go left and up the road to Miller Rocks on the right. There is a trail around the base of the rocks and an easy scramble leads to the top of the rocks, revealing spectacular views west to the Indian Peaks.

Ceran St. Vrain—guide, explorer, fur trader, and fort builder—played an important role in the settling of the wilderness now known as northern Colorado. With his partner, Charles Bent, he founded and built several forts in northern Colorado. Fort St.Vrain, located at the confluence of the South Platte and St. Vrain Rivers is the most famous. He was active in politics, business, and military affairs, and his name will be forever intertwined with the early history and settlement of northern Colorado.

Camping: At the trailhead, along the creek, and near Miller Rocks.

17

Mount Audubon

Highlights: *A wonderful day hike up to the beautiful alpine summit of Mount Audubon (13,223 feet). Wildflowers, panoramic high alpine views, and alpine lakes make this hike well worth the effort. This is a very strenuous hike with a lot of altitude gain in a long, 4.0-mile march to the summit. There are stunning views of Pawnee Peak, Mount Toll, Paiute Peak, Sawtooth Mountain, and Rocky Mountain National Park to the north. This is a very popular trail that sees a fair amount of traffic in the summer months. Your best bet to avoid the crowds would be to do the hike midweek.*

Season: Late June to early October.
Distance: 4.0 miles one way.
Difficulty: Strenuous.
Maps: Trails Illustrated Indian Peaks/Gold Hill #102.

Management: Boulder Ranger District, USDA Forest Service.
Trail conditions: Well-traveled trail on the lower section with very loose, rocky tread to the summit.

Finding the trailhead: From the junction of Colorado Highway 93 and Colorado Highway 119 (Broadway and Canyon) in Boulder, go west on CO 119 for 18 miles to Nederland. Go west on Colorado Highway 72 for 10 miles to County Road 102. Go left on CR 102 to the Brainard Lake Recreation Site ($5.00 admission fee) and the Mitchell Creek Trailhead parking area.

Wildflowers, Mount Audubon

Key points:

0.4 The trail cuts right up a steep switchback.
1.3 Junction with the Beaver Creek Trail.
1.9 Great views of the surrounding peaks and Blue Lake.
2.5 Steep switchbacks.
3.5 Steep switchbacks up to summit.
4.0 Mount Audubon summit.

The hike: The hike starts at the Beaver Creek Trailhead, located at the Mitchell Creek parking area above Brainard Lake. Access the well-marked Beaver Creek Trail on the north side of the parking area. The trail is well maintained and makes a gradual climb to a shelf and the Mount Audubon Trail. After about 0.5 mile of easy hiking through a dense spruce forest, the trail makes a sharp right turn up a steep switchback, with views out to the east. At 1.3 miles the Beaver Creek Trail goes right down to Coney Flats Road. Your trail continues straight. The trail takes a tight line up through a stand of twisted Krummholz pines and a small boulder field. You are gaining considerable altitude at this point, as the pine trees disappear behind you. The trail cuts over a small, beautiful stream and up through a stunning alpine meadow to a snowfield. At 2.5 miles the trail makes a sharp right away from a snowfield and climbs steeply through a boulder field to a broad, flat ridge with excellent views of the surrounding alpine peaks. At 3.5 miles the trail goes left up a steep, rocky trail to the summit. There are a number of trails that shoot off from the main trail and take a steep scramble to the summit. Follow the cairns and stay on the main trail. It is easier to gain the summit following the main trail and less intrusive to the surrounding alpine environment. At 4.0 miles you arrive at the summit of Mount Audubon.

Mount Audubon

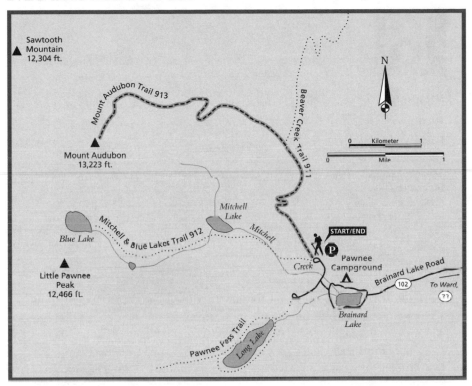

The last section of the hike lies above timberline and is exposed to violent lightning storms. Get an early start and try to be off the summit by noon during the thunderstorm season. The last mile of the trail gains a thousand feet and can be very strenuous for those not acclimated to altitude. Take a break at one of the many rock shelters on the summit and enjoy the spectacular alpine scenery from this beautiful summit. C. C. Parry, a botanist, and zoologist J. W. Velie climbed the mountain in 1864 and named the peak after the famous naturalist, who never set foot in Colorado.

Camping: Brainard Lake Recreation Area.

18

Blue Lake

Highlights: *A wonderful day hike up to Blue Lake in the Indian Peaks Wilderness Area. This short hike takes you up to a beautiful alpine lake surrounded by stunning alpine peaks.*

Season: June to October.
Distance: 2.5 miles one way.
Difficulty: Moderate.
Maps: Trails Illustrated Indian Peaks/
Gold Hill #102.
Management: Boulder Ranger District,
USDA Forest Service.

Trail conditions: Well-traveled and rocky on the lower section with loose, rocky, and wet conditions up to Blue Lake. Expect to find snow on the upper section of the trail well into June.

Finding the trailhead: From the junction of Colorado Highway 93 and Colorado Highway 119 (Broadway and Canyon) in Boulder, go west on CO 119 for 18 miles to Nederland. Go west on Colorado Highway 72 for 10 miles to County Road 102. Go left on CR 102 to the Brainard Lake Recreation Site ($5.00 admission fee) and the Mitchell Creek Trailhead parking area.

Key points:
0.2 Wilderness boundary.
0.8 Mitchell Lake.
1.0 Cross over Mitchell Creek.
1.5 Alpine meadow and ponds.
2.5 Blue Lake.

The hike: This is one of my favorite hikes in the Indian Peaks Wilderness Area, and you get a lot of bang for the buck on this hike. Beautiful views, spectacular wildflowers, lovely alpine lakes; this hike has it all. If you are planning to hike up to Blue Lake during the weekend in the summer month, arrive early to secure a parking space. The parking lot fills up quickly in the summer months and finding a space after early morning can be a problem. The hike begins at the Mitchell Lake Trailhead, located near the restrooms at the Mitchell Lake Trailhead parking area. The Mitchell Lake Trail begins at an elevation of 10,472 feet and climbs to 11,352 feet to Blue Lake in just under 2.5 miles. The start of the trail is wide, level, and somewhat rocky. At the 0.2-mile mark you enter the boundary of the wilderness area and the trail wanders through dense, tall spruce trees. At around the 0.3-mile mark you cross over

Blue Lake

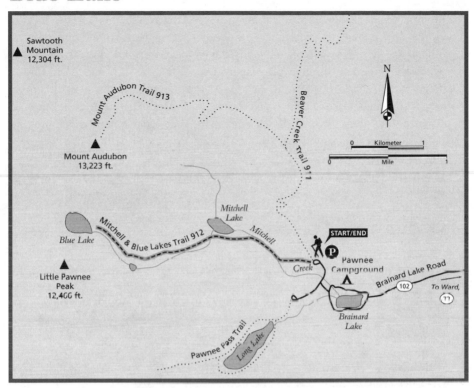

Mitchell Creek on a wood footbridge. After the footbridge the trail climbs gently to Mitchell Lake, with wildflowers and spectacular views of Mount Audubon (13,223 feet), Little Pawnee Peak, Mount Toll, and Paiute Peak. Mitchell Lake is a shallow, fourteen-acre lake that is stocked with cutthroat trout and is quite popular with anglers. The meadow around the lake is filled with wildflowers that grow profusely in the moist, fertile soil. Blanket flowers, alpine primrose, mountain lupines, alpine-avers, golden banner, and globe flowers are just a few of the flowers that blossom around Mitchell Creek and Mitchell Lake. At the 1.0-mile mark the trail crosses over Mitchell Creek again

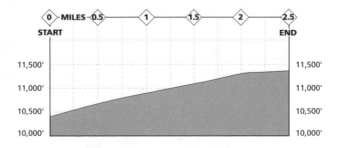

on a makeshift bridge of logs and fallen trees. After Mitchell Creek the trail climbs on log steps to a meadow with good views of the surrounding peaks. This is another place to stop and enjoy the views and the wildflowers. Wood walkways guide you through the marshy area of the meadow and up to the drier, rocky section of the trail. At around the 2.0-mile mark the trail cuts across a snowfield, following rock cairns, with Mitchell Creek and Little Pawnee Peak on the left. At the 2.5-mile mark Blue Lake appears in a cirque below the towering summits of Mount Toll and Paiute Peak. Blue Lake covers almost twenty-three acres, is almost 100 feet deep, and is stocked with cutthroat trout. Take a lunch break and enjoy the panoramic views and alpine splendor.

Camping: Brainard Lake Recreation Area.

19

Heart Lake

Highlights: *A spectacular hike into a beautiful alpine basin, with the main attraction being Heart and Rogers Pass Lakes.*

Season: Early June to late October.
Distance: 4.2 miles one way.
Difficulty: Moderate to strenuous.
Maps: Trails Illustrated Winter Park/Rollins Pass/Central City #103.
Management: Boulder Ranger District, USDA Forest Service.

Trail conditions: The lower section of the Heart Lake Trail has smooth tread and is wet in some spots. The upper section of the trail is wet, very rocky, and filled with roots and scattered downed trees.

Finding the trailhead: From the junction of Colorado Highway 93 and Colorado Highway 119 (Broadway and Canyon) in Boulder, go west on CO 119 for 18 miles to Nederland. Continue on CO 119 for 5.0 miles to

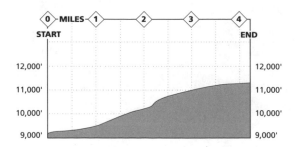

Heart Lake

County Road 149

Rollins Pass Road

South Boulder Creek

East Portal

P

START/END

Forest Lakes Trail 809

Arapaho Creek

South Boulder Creek Trail 900

Arapaho Lakes

Crater Lake

Iceberg Lake

Heart Lake

Rogers Pass Lake

Rogers Pass Trail

Rogers Pass 11,949 ft.

To Rollins Pass

Haystack Mountain 11,622 ft.

James Peak 13,249 ft.

N

Kilometer

Mile

0

1

0

1

Rollinsville. Go right onto County Road 149 for 7.5 miles to a fork in the road. Go left at the fork for 1.0 mile to East Portal and the trailhead.

Key points:
0.4 Arapaho Creek goes off to the right.
0.8 Trail goes right to Forest Lakes.
2.1 Cross over South Boulder Creek.
4.2 Arrive at Heart Lake.

The hike: Heart and Rogers Pass Lakes are situated in an alpine valley below the jagged, rocky summits of Haystack Mountain and James Peak (13,249 feet). The trail to the lakes takes a direct line up a rocky and wet gulch along South Boulder Creek. From the parking area go left over South Boulder Creek just before the Moffat Tunnel to the trailhead and a kiosk. Follow the well-marked trail past the kiosk up along South Boulder Creek. The trail crosses over three wood footbridges over Arapaho Creek up to a meadow that has a pair of abandoned cabins in it. At the meadow there are three wood posts on the trail; to the right is the Forest Lakes Trail. You continue straight and begin a steep climb on rocky, root-filled, wet tread up a rock-infested gully. The trail follows a line along the north side of South Boulder Creek in a dense, mature spruce forest. The spruce trees are draped with moss and the trail follows what was once a mining road. At the 2.1-mile mark the trail becomes level and angles left through an extremely wet section littered with beautiful wildflowers then crosses South Boulder Creek. The trail is somewhat difficult to follow in this section and uses an occasional wood plank to negotiate the wet sections. The trail becomes unclear through this section. Stay near South Boulder Creek and look for red dots on the trees to lead you in the right direction. Past the wet section the trail becomes rocky and steep as you gain altitude on your way up to Heart Lake. You are deep in a dense spruce forest along this section of the trail, but there is an occasional open area that reveals nice views of Nebraska Hill. I hiked this trail in early June, and the upper section of the trail still had a fair amount of snow on it, which made route finding somewhat difficult. At around the 3.8-mile mark the trail comes out of the trees into a beautiful alpine basin, with Haystack Mountain and James Peak on the left. Reach a fork in the trail and go right to Heart Lake. Going to the left will take you to Rogers Pass Lake, Rogers Pass Trail and the Continental Divide. I recommend staying at Heart Lake and spending at least two days exploring this beautiful and remote area.

Camping: At Heart Lake.

20

Heil Valley Ranch/ Lichen Loop

Highlights: *A great family hike in Boulder County's newest open space area. Great way to get the kids out into the woods on a short, scenic loop through stands of beautiful ponderosas and open meadows. Heil Valley Ranch is an excellent spot for wildlife viewing.*

Season: Year-round.
Distance: 1.3-mile loop.
Difficulty: Easy
Maps: Boulder County Open Space/Heil Valley Ranch.

Management: Boulder County Open Space.
Trail conditions: The trail is smooth and is well maintained by volunteers and open space rangers.

Finding the trailhead: From Boulder follow U.S. Highway 36 north toward the town of Lyons to Lefthand Canyon Road. Go left on Lefthand Canyon Road for 0.5 mile to Geer Canyon Road. Go right on Geer Canyon Road for 1.3 miles to the trailhead and parking.

Key points:
0.5 Trail junction.
1.3 End of loop.

The hike: From the trailhead/picnic area reach the kiosk and follow the signs for the Lichen Loop. The trail goes over a wood bridge and heads left up to the start of the loop. Travel through stands of beautiful ponderosas and a meadow filled with tall grasses, yuccas, and cacti. Views to the north up the valley are spectacular, with sharp-cut canyons and open meadows. Reach a trail junction at around the 0.5-mile mark and go right, switchbacking up through the ponderosas. Past several large lichen-covered boulders the trail breaks out into an open meadow with tall prairie grass and the occasional ponderosa tree. Views open to the south and east at upturned sedimentary rock along a ridgeline. The trail cuts through the open meadow and begins a gentle descent back toward the trailhead. Enjoy the pleasant hiking through the meadow and arrive back at the trailhead. Picnic tables are located near the trailhead, so bring a lunch and enjoy spending an afternoon with the family at this beautiful open space area.

Heil Valley Ranch/Lichen Loop

21   Heil Valley Ranch

Highlights: *One of Boulder's best hikes. A beautiful loop high into the foothills through dense stands of ponderosa pines, open meadows with tall prairie grasses, spring wildflowers, and dramatic views north to Mount Meeker (13,911 feet) and Longs Peak (14,255 feet).*

Season: Year-round.
Distance: 8.1-mile loop.
Difficulty: Moderate.
Maps: Boulder County Open Space/Heil Valley Ranch.

Management: Boulder County Open Space.
Trail conditions: The trail is smooth for the most part and is well maintained by volunteers and open space rangers.

Finding the trailhead: From Boulder follow U.S. Highway 36 north toward the town of Lyons to Lefthand Canyon Road. Go left on Lefthand Canyon Road for 0.5 mile to Geer Canyon Road. Go right on Geer Canyon Road for 1.3 miles to the trailhead and parking.

Key points:
0.5 Wapiti Trail.
0.7 Bridge.
1.4 Service road.
1.8 Ruins.
2.7 Ponderosa Loop Trail.
3.5 Service road.
3.9 Overlook.
5.4 Back at the Wapiti Trail.
8.1 Back at the trailhead.

The hike: From the trailhead/picnic area reach the kiosk and follow the sign for the Wapiti Trail. Go left up the short hill and reach a service road. Follow the road north, with excellent views to the north and east. At around the 0.5-mile mark you reach a gate and a spur of the Lichen Loop. Go left on the Wapiti Trail through an open meadow filled with prairie dog mounds. Cross over a bridge and switchback up to an open meadow with open views to the south. Tall prairie grasses are mixed with yuccas, paintbrushes, and cacti. The trail soon enters a dense ponderosa forest and climbs up to a service road. At around the 1.4-mile mark the trail crosses a service road and climbs up through the trees to the remnants of an old stone building. The trail goes left

Heil Valley Ranch

Overlook

Ponderosa Loop Trail

HEIL VALLEY RANCH   OPEN SPACE

Wapiti Trail

Lichen Loop

START/END

Geer Canyon Road

Lefthand Canyon Road

To Lyons

36

To Boulder

N

| 0 | Kilometer | 1 |
| 0 | Mile | 1 |

at the ruins and continues to climb through the ponderosas to a junction with the Ponderosa Loop Trail. At the 2.7-mile mark arrive at the Ponderosa Loop Trail junction. This is a nice spot to take a short break. Go right on the Ponderosa Loop Trail and drop slightly to an open meadow with great views to the north and east. Enjoy open hiking with a southwest exposure. The trail goes back into the ponderosas, much shorter here than on the lower part of the trail, and climbs to a service road. Reach the service road and the 3.5-mile mark, cross the road, and wind back to the north and up to an overlook. Reach the overlook at the 3.9-mile mark and enjoy the dramatic views west to Mount Meeker and Longs Peak, north to St. Vrain Canyon, and east to the open plains. If you packed a lunch, this is the place to stop and eat it. Two benches at the overlook provide a comfortable spot to enjoy lunch and the views. Past the overlook the trail becomes a little rockier and climbs at a gentle grade up to a service road. At around the 4.3-mile mark reach a flat area with amazing view west to Mount Meeker and Longs Peak, at 14,255 feet the highest point in Rocky Mountain National Park. Pass through a section of young ponderosas in a small meadow. The trail now begins to drop back down to the Wapiti Trail. Reach the Wapiti Trail at around the 5.4-mile mark and retrace your route back to the trailhead, with great views to the south and east.

22

Mount Sanitas

Highlights: *A short hike up the Sanitas Valley to the summit of Mount Sanitas (6,863 feet). Once on top of Mount Sanitas you are rewarded with some of the best views to be had in Boulder County. Wildflowers, wildlife, strange rock formations, plus a true summit make for a must-do hike in the Boulder area.*

Season: Year-round. Can be snowy and icy on the north-facing slopes.
Distance: 3.2-mile loop.
Difficulty: Easy to moderate.
Maps: Boulder County, USGS, and Boulder County Open Space/Mount Sanitas.

Management: City of Boulder Mountain Parks and Open Space.
Trail conditions: The trail is smooth on the way up the valley and becomes rocky to the summit and back down to the trailhead.

Finding the trailhead: From Broadway and Mapleton Avenue in Boulder, travel west on Mapleton for 0.8 mile to the Mount Sanitas Trailhead and parking area on the right and left side of the road.

Key points:
1.0 Kiosk.
1.8 Summit of Mount Sanitas.
3.2 Back at the parking area.

The hike: From the parking area skirt the day-pavilion and head right to a wide dirt road. Go left and up the road, beginning a gradual climb up the Sanitas Valley. Pass the Dakota Ridge Trail on the right and continue straight to the north. The road you are hiking on was once a wagon road used to access various quarries in the Sanitas Valley. At around the 0.9-mile mark the Hawthorne Trail goes right and down. You go left and up the road past a kiosk. The trail soon narrows and begins switchbacking up the east side of Mount

Mount Sanitas

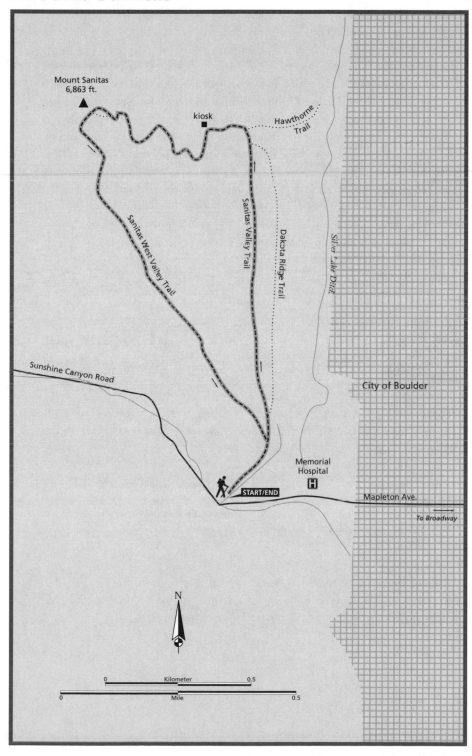

Mount Sanitas
6,863 ft.

kiosk

Hawthorne Trail

Sanitas Valley Trail

Dakota Ridge Trail

Sanitas West Valley Trail

Silver Lake Ditch

Sunshine Canyon Road

City of Boulder

Memorial Hospital
H

START/END

Mapleton Ave.

To Broadway

N

0   Kilometer   0.5
0   Mile   0.5

Sanitas. Cacti, Indian paintbrushes, and other wildflowers grow profusely on this open hillside during the late spring and summer months. The trail drops across a small gulch, then begins to climb in earnest through the rocks to the summit of Mount Sanitas. Arrive at the summit and take a well-deserved rest. Enjoy the views east to the plains and the city of Boulder. The loop now drops steeply down the west side of Mount Sanitas and you lose elevation quickly. The trail is extremely rocky and can be quite icy in the winter months. At around the 2.3-mile mark the trail parallels short sandstone rock formations on the left. Rock climbers use these cliffs to hone their climbing skills, and the cliffs have become quite popular in recent years. The trail now drops on very loose and rocky log and rock steps and winds around the rocks back toward the trailhead. Cross over a small wood bridge and go right to the pavilion and the end of the hike. This is an extremely popular area with trail users and can be very crowded on weekends and late afternoons. Arrive early or in the middle of the afternoon to secure a parking place.

23 Bald Mountain Scenic Area

Highlights: *As the name suggests, this is a short, scenic hike around and up to the top of Bald Mountain (7,160 feet). There are spectacular views of the Indian Peaks and the plains. Great hike for the young ones.*

Season: Year-round.
Distance: 1.5-mile loop.
Difficulty: Easy.
Maps: Boulder County, USGS, and Boulder County Open Space/Bald Mountain.

Management: City of Boulder Mountain Parks and Open Space.
Trail conditions: The trail is smooth.

Finding the trailhead: From Broadway and Mapleton Avenue in Boulder, travel west on Mapleton and Sunshine Canyon Road for 4.8 miles to the Bald Mountain Scenic Area trailhead and parking area on the left.

Key points:
0.2 Trail forks.
0.9 Top of Bald Mountain.
1.5 Back at the trailhead.

Bald Mountain Scenic Area

START/END

Sunshine Canyon Road

To Boulder

N

Kilometer
Mile
0.5
0.5
0
0

Summit Trail

Pines-to-Peak Trail

Bald Mountain
7,160 ft.

Gulch

Shortcut

The hike: What a great hike to bring the kids on! It's short, there are numerous places to stop, there are picnic tables located near the trailhead, and the views are just spectacular. From the parking area the trail travels past an old corral and several picnic tables on a smooth, wide trail to a trail junction. The Summit Trail goes up and to the left. You go right on the Pines-to-Peak Trail and curve to the west. The trail parallels Sunshine Canyon Road for a short distance through a small stand of ponderosa pines. Expect to see wildflowers during the late spring and summer months along this section of the trail. The trail winds to the south and you are faced with breathtaking views of the southern Indian Peaks. North and South Arapaho Peaks stand tall in the southern skyline and you get a full view of Arapaho Glacier, the southernmost glacier in North America. At around the 0.6-mile mark the trail goes back to the east through a stand of ponderosa and lodgepole pines, with a bench on the right. Continue east into an open meadow, where the trail to the summit goes up and left. There are lots of wildflowers here during the summer months. Make a short climb, with open views in all directions, to the summit, where a bench nestles in a cluster of ponderosa pines. Take a break and enjoy the views. The trail now drops down through the ponderosas and curves back to the east toward the trailhead. The trail passes several stately ponderosas and meets the Pines-to-Peak Trail again. Go left and back to the trailhead. Be on the lookout for mule deer, Abert squirrels, chipmunks, Nuttall's cottontails, magpies, and other wildlife. The corral and cattle chute near the trailhead are the remains of an old homestead from the late 1800s. Mining was done near the Bald Mountain Scenic Area, and remnants of the old Weist Brothers mines can be seen around Bald Mountain.

Betasso Preserve

Highlights: *The city of Boulder and the county of Boulder have done an amazing job of preserving lands in and around the city and Betasso Preserve is one of the many open space lands that citizens of Boulder County and the Front Range can use to recreate. This hike is a nice outing through forests of ponderosa pines on a smooth well-maintained trail.*

Season: Year-round.
Distance: 3.2-mile loop.
Difficulty: Easy.
Maps: Boulder County Open Space/Betasso Preserve.

Management: Boulder County Open Space.
Trail conditions: The trail is smooth and is well maintained by volunteers and open space rangers.

Finding the trailhead: From the junction of Colorado Highway 93 and Colorado Highway 119 (Broadway and Canyon) in Boulder, go west on CO 119 toward Nederland. Go right on Sugarloaf Road and travel 0.8 mile to the turnoff for Betasso Preserve. Go right and follow signs to the trailhead, picnic area, and parking.

Key points:
0.1 Gate.
0.2 Canyon LoopTrail.
1.6 Creek crossing.
1.9 Second creek crossing.
2.8 Gate.
3.2 Back at the trailhead.

The hike: From the trailhead/picnic area go left on the Canyon Loop Trail. Climb a short hill, with excellent views to the west. Reach the top of the hill and follow the trail through the trees and down. The trail drops through the trees and at around the 0.8-mile mark climbs up a short hill, covered with beautiful wildflowers during the summer months. The trail goes right and switchbacks down to a small creek crossing. At around the 1.9-mile mark make a second creek crossing and begin a gentle climb through the trees.

This area was first homesteaded by the Blanchard family, who worked the land for a number of years and in 1915 sold the ranch to Steve Betasso. The Betasso family raised cattle on the land for sixty years and in 1975 sold the land

Betasso Preserve

To Boulder

119

N

Kilometer
Mile

Fourmile Canyon Road

Fourmile Creek

6,326 ft.

119

Canyon Loop Trail

Betasso
Preserve

Bummer's
Rock

Creek

P
START/END

Boulder

Sugarloaf Road

To Nederland

to Boulder County to be preserved as open space. Remnants of the old homestead can be seen scattered along the trail and near the picnic area.

Continue on the smooth trail and up to a gate. Numerous volunteers and open space rangers put in many an hour working on the trail and bringing it to its present standard. Thanks to all these folks for their hard work and a job well done. At around the 2.8-mile mark you reach a gate and an old road. Follow the road back to the trailhead and picnic area. Bring the family, pack a lunch, and enjoy this beautiful piece of open space.

Sugarloaf Mountain

Highlights: *A short hike up to the top of Sugarloaf Mountain (8,912 feet), with spectacular views of the Indian Peaks Wilderness, Rocky Mountain National Park, James Peak Wilderness Area, and the plains. Sunsets and sunrises on top of Sugarloaf Mountain are not to be missed. Doing the hike at these times will reward you with a beautiful show of nature's light.*

Season: Year-round.
Distance: 1.1 miles one way.
Difficulty: Moderate.
Maps: Trails Illustrated Indian Peaks/Gold Hill #104.

Management: Boulder County Parks.
Trail conditions: The trail follows an old, rocky mining road.

Finding the trailhead: From the junction of Colorado Highway 93 and Colorado Highway 119 (Broadway and Canyon) in Boulder, go west on CO 119 for 5.5 miles to Sugarloaf Road. Turn right on Sugarloaf Road and travel 4.5 miles to a turnoff on the right for the Switzerland Trailhead. Go right for 1.0 mile up to the trailhead and a parking area. The hike starts here.

Sugarloaf Mountain

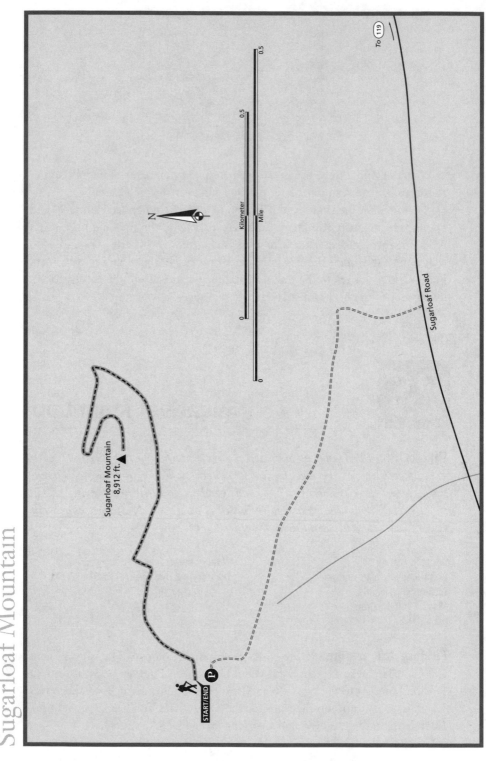

Sugarloaf Mountain
8,912 ft.

N

Kilometer
Mile

0   0.5
0   0.5

START/END
P

To 119

Sugarloaf Road

Key points:

0.6 Switchbacks.

0.8 Sugarloaf Mountain sign on the left.

1.1 Top of Sugarloaf Mountain.

The hike: From the parking area look to the east for an old road with two metal posts and a cable going across it. Travel up the road past the cable and begin climbing on the rough old road. Ponderosa pines, Douglas firs, and small aspen trees line the trail through this section. From Boulder the top of Sugarloaf Mountain looks stark and barren, but that's not the case here on the western side of the mountain, which is covered by various trees and wildflowers. Continue up to the first of several switchbacks that force the trail to the east and south. At around the 0.8-mile mark you pass a sign on the left. Here are the first indications of the Sugarloaf fire, which charred many acres on the east and south sides of the mountain. Burned and twisted pines are scattered along the steep slope of the mountain and give an eerie feel to this section of the trail. The trail cuts straight across a scree slope and makes a sharp left up to the summit. Spectacular views of the Indian Peaks and Rocky Mountain National Park smack you right in the face at the sharp turn and makes a good reason to stop and enjoy. Heading back west, the trail soon gains the summit and you are rewarded with spectacular views in all directions. If you time your hike right and arrive around sunset, you will enjoy a beautiful show and breathtaking light. Enjoy the views before heading back down the trail to the parking area.

26

Gregory Canyon
Green Mountain Loop

Highlights: *Another gem in Boulder Mountain Park. A great outing up a beautiful canyon with views to the east, west, and north.*

Season: Year-round.
Distance: 3.1-mile loop.
Difficulty: Moderate to strenuous.
Maps: Eldorado Springs 7.5.

Management: City of Boulder Mountain Parks and Open Space.
Trail conditions: The trail is rocky and steep for most of the loop.

Finding the trailhead: From Broadway and Baseline Road in Boulder, go west on Baseline (toward Flagstaff Mountain) for 1.4 miles to the Gregory Canyon Trailhead and parking.

Key points:
1.2 Green Mountain Lodge and E. M. Greenman Trail
1.7 Saddle Rock Trail.
3.1 Back at the trailhead.

The hike: From the parking area/trailhead follow the sign for the Gregory Canyon Trail, heading west through thick vegetation. Within a short distance you will arrive at a junction with the Saddle Rock Trail on the left. This is the return loop at the end of the hike. Bear right, following the Gregory Canyon Trail and climbing at a modest grade. Good views of sandstone rocks appear, with lush vegetation down and to the left along the drainage. The trail becomes rocky the higher you climb, with great views back to Boulder and the east. After a mile and 900 feet of elevation gain, the trail reaches a ridge and skirts through a beautiful forest of ponderosa pine and Douglas fir. Make a small drop to a stream on the left and an old road on the right. This lovely, small, open meadow has beautiful, large ferns and alpine flowers blooming

Gregory Canyon

City of Boulder

Broadway

Baseline Road

Gregory Creek

START/END

N

kilometer

Mile

Saddle Rock Trail

Gregory Canyon Trail

Green Mountain 8,144 ft.

Greer Mountain Lodge

E. M. Greenman Trail

Flagstaff Road

Long Canyon Trail

along the trail in the summer months. Go left up to the Green Mountain Lodge, a restroom, a picnic table, a kiosk, and a trail junction. Here you follow the E. M. Greenman Trail up into a forest of ponderosa and lodgepole pines. The trail becomes quite narrow and rocky, climbing steeply to a junction with the Saddle Rock Trail at 1.7 miles into the hike. Go left onto the Saddle Rock Trail (going right for 1.3 miles will take you to the top of Green Mountain—8,144 feet) along rocky tread with views back west to the Indian Peaks and north to Mount Meeker (13,911 feet) and Longs Peak (14,255 feet). At the 1.9-mile mark the trail drops quite dramatically into Gregory Canyon. Certain portions of the trail are very steep, so use caution when descending. There are great views again to the east, with a spectacular view of the University of Colorado campus and the plains. At the 2.7-mile mark the trail makes a sharp right along a small drainage and drops steeply back to the parking area to complete the loop. This is a very popular trail and sees a lot of use by hikers, trail runners, and bird watchers. Dogs are allowed but must be kept on a leash or under strict voice command. Do not cut switchbacks or make new trails, and yield to the uphill hiker.

27

Bear Peak

Highlights: *A strenuous but great hike up the summit of Bear Peak (8,461 feet), one of Boulder's most visible landmarks. The Bear Peak Trail follows Bear Creek up beautiful Bear Canyon, then makes a steep ascent up the Bear Peak West Ridge Trail to the summit of Bear Peak. Expect beautiful vistas and blooming wildflowers during the summer months.*

Season: Year-round.
Distance: 7.4-mile loop.
Difficulty: Strenuous.
Maps: Eldorado Springs 7.5.
Management: City of Boulder Mountain Parks and Open Space.

Trail conditions: Well-traveled and smooth going up to the Bear Canyon Trail. From there on the trail is rocky and steep.

Finding the trailhead: From Broadway and Table Mesa Road in Boulder, go west on Table Mesa for 2.4 miles to the National Center for Atmospheric Research (NCAR), parking, and the trailhead.

View from Bear Peak

Key points:

0.2 Kiosk and sign for the Mesa Trail.
0.7 Water tank.
1.2 Junction with the Mesa Trail and Bear Creek.
1.4 Junction with Bear Canyon Trail.
3.1 Junction with Green-Bear Trail.
4.7 Summit of Bear Peak.
4.8 Junction with Fern Canyon Trail.
5.6 Junction with Shanahan North Trail.
6.0 Junction with Mesa Trail.
7.4 Back at NCAR and the parking area.

The hike: From the parking area, access the Walter Orr–Roberts Weather Trail on the west side of NCAR. Follow this informative trail for a short 0.2 mile to a kiosk and a sign pointing to the Mesa Trail. Drop a short distance,

Bear Peak

N

0 — 1 Kilometer
0 — 1 Mile

Broadway

City of Boulder

Table Mesa Road

National Center for
Atmospheric Research

START/END

Bear Creek

Walter Orr–Roberts
Weather Trail

Mesa Trail

Shanahan North Trail

Mesa Trail

Mallory
Cave Trail

Bear Canyon Trail

Bear Canyon

Fern Canyon Trail

Bear Peak
8,461 ft.

South Boulder Peak
8,549 ft.

Green–Bear Trail

Bear Creek

Bear Peak West Ridge Trail

then climb steeply to a water tower. From the water tower follow signs for the Mesa Trail, staying left at all trail junctions. At the 1.2-mile mark you arrive at the junction of Mesa Trail and Bear Creek. Go left up the steep, wide road to a junction with the Bear Canyon Trail on the right. Go right, passing a utility tower and powerlines. The trail becomes rockier and begins to climb steeply. The trail crosses Bear Creek several times and winds through several patches of aspens, willows, and cottonwoods. Wildflowers grow profusely along the creek, as do ferns and other flowering shrubs. At the 3.1-mile mark you arrive at a beautiful, small meadow and a trail junction. The Green-Bear Trail goes to the right. You go left and up on the Bear Peak West Ridge Trail into the pines. The trail climbs steeply through the pines to an open area at an old fenceline. The trail cuts to the left and away from private property. Here views open to the west to Walker Ranch Open Space, the Indian Peaks, and Mount Meeker (13,911) to the north. The trail begins to climb a steep hillside with numerous granite boulders. At around the 4.2-mile mark the trail forks to the left, climbing a series of steep, granite steps. Before you know it you are standing below the pointed summit of Bear Peak. Follow the trail through the rocks to the north ridge past the Fern Canyon Trail and scramble up the north ridge to the summit proper. Take a long rest and enjoy the spectacular views in all directions. After your rest and photo session, go back down the ridge to the Fern Canyon Trail. Go right and down the very steep Fern Canyon Trail to a saddle. The trail is loose and rocky and drops over 2,000 feet in 1.4 miles, a real knee tweaker. Fern Canyon is a densely vegetated, narrow canyon filled with spectacular rock formations, aspens, and pine trees. The trail in several sections is made of steep steps and wood stairs. The trail breaks out of the narrow canyon and you arrive at a junction with Shanahan North Trail. Continue straight on the Fern Canyon Trail, dropping to the Mesa Trail. Wildflowers bloom along the trail and the open areas. Go left on the Mesa Trail down to Bear Creek. From here retrace your route back to NCAR and the parking area.

28 Meyers Homestead Trail

Highlights: *A peaceful hike along an old fire road, past an old homestead, and through open meadows and stands of ponderosas, Douglas firs, and quaking aspens.*

Season: Year-round.
Distance: 2.6 miles one way.
Difficulty: Moderate.

Maps: Boulder County Open Space/Walker Ranch.
Management: Boulder County Open Space.
Trail conditions: Smooth.

Finding the trailhead: From the intersection of Broadway and Baseline Road in Boulder, travel west on Baseline then Flagstaff Road for 7.5 miles to the Meyers Open Space parking area on the right. The hike starts here.

Key points:

0.5 Meyers Homestead.
1.3 Road junction.
1.8 Aspen forest.
2.6 Overlook and turnaround point.

The hike: From the parking area access the wide Meyers Homestead Trail near the kiosk. Follow the trail down into an open meadow. Remnants of a recent fire can be seen on the hillside to the left. The trail drops into a narrow meadow, with the old Meyers Homestead on the left. The homestead is all that is left of a thriving cattle ranch from the late 1800s. Past the homestead the trail climbs a short hill, with a small stream on the left. Thick willows line the banks of the stream, along with aspens and other water-loving plants. The hillside on the right of the trail is covered with granite boulders, widely spaced ponderosas, and blooming wildflowers (during the summer months). The trail reaches an old fire road at the 1.3-mile mark and then climbs a short steep hill. Pleasant hiking leads you up past a steep, forested hillside on the left and open

Meyers Homestead Trail

To Baseline Road, Boulder

□ overlook

Flagstaff Road

Meyers Homestead Trail

Meyers Homestead ■

START/END

P

Gross Reservoir

Columbine Gulch Trail

Eldorado Canyon Trail

To Eldorado State Park

South Boulder Creek

Reservoir Road

Crescent Meadow Trail

N

| 0 | Kilometer | 1 |
| 0 | Mile | 1 |

area on the right to a beautiful young aspen forest at the 1.8-mile mark. The trail climbs steeply through the aspens and reaches a beautiful open meadow at the 2.1-mile mark. Enter into the meadow filled with tall grasses; there is a small stream lined with willows and aspen trees on the left. The meadow is also filled with various wildflowers during the summer months and is a great spot to take a break and enjoy the serene setting. The trail climbs at a gentle grade through the meadow, then reaches a flat area at the crest of the hill. Great views open to the north and east to Boulder. The trail heads sharply to the left and soon reaches the overlook and the turnaround point of the hike. Enjoy the views of Sugarloaf Mountain (8,912 feet) and Boulder Canyon. After a short break turn around and retrace your route to the trailhead.

Walker Ranch

Highlights: *A popular hike around the old homestead of James Walker. Beautiful views, excellent wildflowers, and good fishing along South Boulder Creek are the main attractions on this hike. Fly-fishing is excellent along several sections of South Boulder Creek.*

Season: Year-round.
Distance: 7.4-mile loop.
Difficulty: Moderate.
Maps: Boulder County, USGS, and Boulder County Open Space/Walker Ranch.

Management: City of Boulder Mountain Parks and Open Space.
Trail conditions: The trail is extremely rocky in places.

Finding the trailhead: From Boulder at the intersection of Broadway and Baseline Road, travel 7.5 miles west on Baseline then Flagstaff Road up past Flagstaff Mountain. Turn left into the South Boulder Creek Trailhead and parking area.

Walker Ranch

overlook

Flagstaff Road

To Baseline Road, Boulder

Meyers Homestead Trail

Meyers Homestead ■

START/END

Cross Reservoir

South Boulder Creek

Columbine Gulch Trail

Eldorado Canyon Trail

To Eldorado State Park

Reservoir Road

Crescent Meadow Trail

N

| 0 | Kilometer | 1 |
| 0 | Mile | 1 |

Key points:
1.0 Small stream crossing.
1.5 Bridge over South Boulder Creek.
2.4 Reservoir Road.
4.5 Steep, rocky descent.
4.7 Bridge.
5.8 Columbine Gulch Trail.
7.4 Back at the trailhead.

The hike: From the trailhead go through the gate and begin a nice descent to South Boulder Creek. The trail follows an old road and passes several rock formations on the right. At the bottom of the hill, cross a small stream and then go right along beautiful South Boulder Creek. The trail goes upstream to a bridge. Cross the bridge and go left up the steep hill. Crest the steep part of the hill where the trail bends to the right and enjoy excellent views to the west. This trail is extremely popular with mountain bikers, so be aware of their presence, especially on weekends. The trail becomes level just past a small rock garden and travels past a gate and down through a beautiful forested area. Climb up a hill and through another gate, where the trail drops you on to Reservoir Road. Go left up the road for 0.1 mile to a trail on the left. Go left up the trail and arrive at Crescent Meadows. Go left on a narrow trail heading to the east and through the open meadow. There are great views to the west, and wildflowers light up the meadow in late spring and early summer. At around the 3.5-mile mark the trail leads you into a dense forest and starts to drop in elevation. Travel past several rocky sections and through a small, open meadow. Arrive at a sign warning mountain bikers to dismount. Follow rock-and-log steps steeply down to South Boulder Creek and a bridge. This is a good spot to take a break and admire the scenery. South Boulder Creek runs wild through this section, and the deep pools of water are crystal clear and are excellent for fly-fishing. Cross the bridge and go left, passing the Eldorado Canyon Trail on the right. Begin a good climb through the ponderosa and spruce trees to a junction with the Columbine Gulch Trail at the 5.8-mile mark. Go left on this narrow trail into a narrow, forested gulch. Pass a small stream, then begin a steep ascent past several switchbacks. A beautiful hike brings you up and out of the gulch to a ridge and excellent views. Go right and up a gentle grade, following the obvious trail past a recent burn area back to the trailhead.

Once the site of the largest cattle ranch on the Front Range, Walker Ranch is now a beautiful piece of open space land that provides a glimpse into Boulder County history. James Walker first came to the area for health reasons and thrived in the fresh mountain air and peaceful setting of open meadows and mountain terrain. Hope you do the same on this hike.

30 Walden Ponds Wildlife Area

Highlights: *A wonderful family hike around several ponds, with spectacular views of the Indian Peaks. The boardwalk along Cottonwood Marsh has several interpretive signs and is a great place to bring the kids for an educational hike. Walden Ponds is also a stopover for migratory birds and offers a great opportunity to view waterfowl, songbirds, and various mammals.*

Season: Year-round.
Distance: 2.1-mile loop.
Difficulty: Easy.
Maps: Boulder County Open Space/Walden Ponds.

Management: Boulder County Open Space.
Trail conditions: The trail is smooth and is well maintained by volunteers and open space rangers.

Finding the trailhead: From the intersection of U.S. Highway 36 (28th Street) and Colorado Highway 7 (Arapahoe Avenue) in Boulder, travel east on CO 7 for 5.0 miles to 75th Street. Go left on 75th Street for 2.0 miles to the entrance of Walden Ponds Open Space. Turn left and travel 0.2 mile to the Cottonwood Marsh picnic area and trailhead.

Key points:
0.2 Sawmill Ponds.
0.9 Bear left at fence line.
1.7 Go left at viewing blind.
2.1 Back at the trailhead.

The hike: The hike starts at the Cottonwood Marsh picnic area and quickly accesses the boardwalk, which has several interpretive signs explaining the geology and history of the area. The boardwalk cuts through a marshy area with tall cattails and thick marsh grasses. After the boardwalk the trail soon meets a service road and travels up toward the ranger field station. Go left up through a fence line to a kiosk and the first of the Sawmill Ponds. Go right at the kiosk and begin the start of the loop around Sawmill Ponds. Be on the lookout for waterfowl and high-flying raptors. Fishing is permitted in the ponds, and several sidetrails access the ponds off the main trail. The trail now goes west, with amazing views of the majestic Indian Peaks. Pelican Marsh, Island Lake, and Bass Pond are on your right. Trails access this area, so if you have the time feel free to explore. At around the 0.9-mile mark the trail goes to the left and into a stand of tall cottonwoods and thick Russian olive trees.

Walden Ponds is in a constant state of flux, and a huge effort has been put

Walden Ponds Wildlife Area

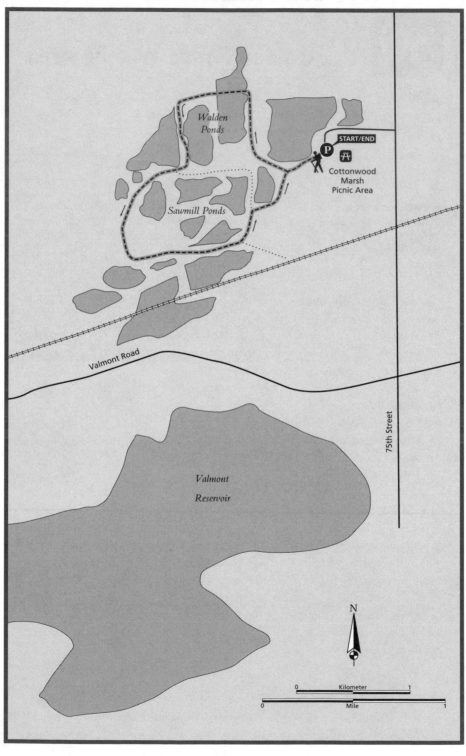

Walden Ponds

Sawmill Ponds

START/END

Cottonwood Marsh Picnic Area

Valmont Road

75th Street

Valmont Reservoir

N

| 0 | Kilometer | 1 |
| 0 | Mile | 1 |

Walden Ponds Wildlife Area

forth to restore the area to its natural state. Once the site of a gravel operation
for the county of Boulder, as little as thirty years ago the land at Walden Ponds
was open pits and stagnant, still water. In 1974 Boulder County, with support
from citizens, started an aggressive program of reclamation. Pit runs were
shaped and formed into ponds and small islands. Water was diverted to establish
ponds, and tree and shrub seedlings were planted to enhance natural vegetation.
What you see today is an ongoing effort to create a viable and aesthetically
pleasing plant and wildlife habitat. Tall marsh grasses, cattails, and muskrat dens
are off to the left. A large, sun-bleached cottonwood on the right is a favorite

perch for birds of prey. Keep an eye open for these beautiful birds that prey on the small rodents and cottontail rabbits that call Walden Ponds home.

At around the 1.5-mile mark the trail curves back to the east toward a viewing blind. Go left at the blind and follow the trail along a fence line, with Duck Pond on your right. Back at the kiosk retrace your route back to the picnic area and the parking lot.

31

Marshall Mesa

Highlights: *A nice short hike with beautiful views of the Indian Peaks, the Flatirons, Mount Meeker (13,911 feet) and Longs Peak (14,255 feet). This is a nice hike for the whole family, with interpretive signs along the trail that explain geology and local history. Coyotes, deer, raptors, and other wildlife call Marshall Mesa home.*

Season: Year-round.
Distance: 2.3-mile loop.
Difficulty: Easy.
Maps: Boulder County Open Space/Marshall Mesa.

Management: Boulder County Open Space.
Trail conditions: The trail is smooth and is well maintained by volunteers and open space rangers.

Finding the trailhead: From the intersection of Broadway and Table Mesa Drive in Boulder, travel south on Broadway to Colorado Highway 170 (Marshall Drive). Turn left on CO 170 to the Marshall Mesa Trailhead parking lot on the right.

Marshall Mesa

To Boulder

170

Marshall

START/END

Marshall Mesa

Community Ditch

Community
Ditch Trail

Marshall
Lake

93

Green Belt Plateau Trail

N

128

To Golden

| 0 | Kilometer | 1 |
| 0 | Mile | 1 |

Key points:
0.1 Bridge.
0.5 Top of hill.
1.5 Trail junction.
2.3 Back at the trailhead.

The hike: This is an extremely popular hike, and for good reason. The trail is well maintained, the vistas are beautiful, and the trail is conveniently located between U.S. Highway 36 and Colorado Highway 93. The trailhead parking area fills up quickly on the weekends, so plan on arriving early. From the trailhead go through the gate on the wide dirt trail. A kiosk is located at the trailhead, as are plastic bags for dog droppings. Take the time to read the information on the kiosk, and a bag if you brought a dog. Past the kiosk the trail climbs gently up a footbridge. Past the footbridge the trail forks. Go left along the irrigation ditch. The trail climbs at a modest grade and contours around the side of a beautiful hill covered with tall grasses and wildflowers in the summer months. The first of the interpretive signs is located half way up the hill. At the 0.5-mile mark you reach the top of the hill and are rewarded with spectacular views to the west. Take a break and enjoy the splendor. Go right and follow the wide trail to Community Ditch. At around the 0.7-mile mark the trail meets the ditch and heads west. The trail going to the right leads to the privately owned Marshall Lake. Continue along the level trail, with wonderful views of the rocky, tilted Flatirons.

Marshall Mesa and the surrounding lands were heavily mined in the late 1800s and early 1900s. Numerous coal mines were worked in the area, producing coal for towns in Boulder and Denver Counties. The area thrived, and at one time more than 800 residents called Marshall home; the town had more residents than Boulder in the late 1800s.

At around the 1.4-mile mark you come to a gate. Close the gate behind you and travel a short distance to a trail junction. Go right at the junction and pass through another gate. Close the gate behind you. Begin a gradual downhill back toward the trailhead through stands of beautiful ponderosas. Several interpretive signs are located along the trail and are a good reason to prolong the hike. Drop down through juniper, ponderosas, and oak bushes back to a familiar trail junction. Cross over the footbridge and scramble back to the trailhead.

32

Doudy Draw Trail

Highlights: *A beautiful hike up a wide draw filled with tall prairie grasses, western wheatgrass, yuccas, wildflowers, ponderosa pines, and cottonwood trees with spectacular views of the Flatirons.*

Season: Year-round. Can be extremely muddy after any precipitation.
Distance: 3.4 miles one way.
Difficulty: Easy to moderate.

Maps: Boulder County, USGS, and City of Boulder Open Space/Doudy Draw.
Management: Colorado State Parks.
Trail conditions: The trail is mostly smooth and free of rocks.

Finding the trailhead: From the intersection of Broadway and Baseline in Boulder, travel south on Broadway (Colorado Highway 93) to Colorado Highway 170. Go right on CO 170 for 1.5 miles to the Doudy Draw Trailhead and parking area on the left.

Key points:
0.4 Picnic area.
0.5 Trail junction.
1.6 Start of the hill.
3.4 Flatirons Vista Trailhead.

The hike: From the parking area pass through a gate and travel up the paved, handicap-accessed trail to the Doudy Draw picnic area. Travel past the picnic area on the left and the restrooms on the right over a small creek lined with thick cottonwood trees. These water-loving trees are quite beautiful and in the fall add dramatic golden color to the already colorful landscape. At around the 0.5-mile mark the Community Ditch Trail comes in from the right just before a bridge. The Community Ditch Trail goes to the east along the ditch up to CO 93. Continue straight over the bridge and through the first gate. Please close the gate behind you. Drop to a seasonal stream crossing. Willows, wild-flowers, and tall prairie grasses grow along the creek and are quite beautiful during the late spring and early summer months. The trail travels up an open area past two gates, with dramatic views to the west and the Flatirons. Looking directly west to Eldorado Canyon, you can catch a quick glimpse of the tall peaks along the Continental Divide. Past the third gate the trail cuts across the creek and starts to climb into the ponderosas to a ridge. Follow a long switch-back to the ridge and enjoy shaded hiking through the ponderosa. The trail

Doudy Draw Trail

To Boulder

Marshall Mesa

Eldorado Springs Drive

Mesa Trail

Community Ditch

Community Ditch Trail

Doudy Draw
Trailhead

START/END

To Eldorado Springs

93

Doudy Draw Trail

Flatirons Vista
Trailhead

126

N

0   Kilometer   1
0   Mile   1

To Golden

becomes a little rocky; looking back, the views become more open to the west and north. This section of the trail marks the border of prairie grassland and the forest. The hiking is level and enjoyable as you pass under power lines. Reach an open area around the 2.6-mile mark where the trail turns into an old service road. Follow the road, with views to the east, south, and north. The trail soon drops to the Flatirons Vista Trailhead and the turnaround point of this hike. Retrace your route to the Doudy Draw Trailhead and enjoy downhill hiking with fantastic views to the west and north.

33 Rattlesnake Gulch

Highlights: *A short, steep hike up a beautiful, narrow gulch, with views of towering rock walls and the Indian Peaks in beautiful Eldorado Canyon State Park.*

Season: Year-round. Can be snowy and icy on the north-facing slopes.
Distance: 5.3-mile loop.
Difficulty: Easy to moderate.
Maps: Boulder County, USGS, and Colorado State Parks/Eldorado Canyon State Park.

Management: Colorado State Parks.
Trail conditions: The start of the hike follows a dirt road and then becomes rocky up Rattlesnake Gulch.

Finding the trailhead: From the intersection of Broadway and Baseline in Boulder, travel south on Broadway (Colorado Highway 93) to Colorado Highway 170. Go right on CO 170 for 4.4 miles to the entrance station and parking area for Eldorado Canyon State Park. Admission is $4.00.

Key points:
0.6 Fowler Trail.
0.8 Rattlesnake Gulch Trail.

2.0 Old hotel ruins.
2.7 Go left.
4.7 Fowler Trail.
5.3 Back at the parking area.

The hike: Eldorado Canyon State Park is located 7.0 miles from downtown Boulder and offers great outdoor recreation and spectacular scenery close to an ever-encroaching urban area. This is one of two hikes in Eldorado Canyon State Park that are great little getaways offering year-round hiking in a beautiful state park. From the parking area/fee station head west up the dirt road. Pass a towering rock wall on the left: the Bastille. Take time to look at any rock climbers, then continue straight up the road, with South Boulder Creek on your right. Gold and brown rock walls are on the right and offer some of the best rock climbing in America. At the 0.6-mile mark go left on the Fowler Trail. After a short distance go right on the Rattlesnake Gulch Trail and climb at a gentle grade on a narrow rocky trail into a V-shaped gulch filled with aspens, willows, and wildflowers. Cross over a seasonal creek and begin a steep climb up the east side of the gulch on a rocky, narrow trail. The trail switchbacks up the hill and then reaches an open area, with views to the north, east, and west. Travel a short distance and reach the remains of the old Crags Hotel, built in the early 1900s. The hotel was reached via train or tramway and was in operation for four years before burning down. Only the foundation of the hotel remains to tell the tale of a once popular getaway for tourists. Pass the remains and travel through a forest of Douglas firs and ponderosa pines. At around the 2.3-mile mark the trail splits, go left and up the narrow trail into the pines. The trail curves back east and then meets with the main trail at around the 2.7-mile mark. Go left and begin a steep descent back down Rattlesnake Gulch. On the way back to the road, if you have the time, follow the Fowler Trail to the east and to the back side of the Bastille. Interpretive signs are located along the trail, as are benches to take a break and look at the rock climbers scaling their way up the vertical walls. A climber's trail goes down the west side of the Bastille and will drop you on the road a short distance from the parking area. Go right back to the parking area.

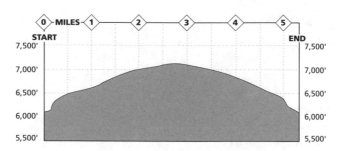

Rattlesnake Gulch

South Boulder Peak
8,549 ft.

Walker Ranch

Eldorado Canyon Trail

North Draw

Shirt Tail Peak
7,240 ft.

ELDORADO CANYON
STATE PARK

South Boulder Creek

Eldorado Springs

170

Pay Station

Fowler Trail

START/END

P

P

Rattlesnake Gulch Trail

N

Kilometer

Mile

34

Eldorado Canyon Trail

Highlights: *A beautiful hike along towering rock walls. The trail travels up a south- and west-facing hillside through North Draw with spectacular views of the Indian Peaks, the Continental Divide, Denver, and towering, sheer rock walls.*

Season: Year-round.
Distance: 2.9 miles one way.
Difficulty: Moderate.
Maps: Boulder County, USGS, and Colorado State Parks/Eldorado Canyon State Park.

Management: Colorado State Parks.
Trail conditions: The trail can be quite smooth and extremely rocky.

Finding the trailhead: From the intersection of Broadway and Baseline in Boulder, travel south on Broadway (Colorado Highway 93) to Colorado Highway 170. Go right on CO 170 for 4.4 miles to the entrance fee station and parking area for Eldorado Canyon State Park. Pay the $4.00 admission day fee and follow the dirt road up to the ranger station and parking area. The hike starts here.

Key points:
0.5 Climbers' trail to Ricon Wall.
0.9 Eldorado Canyon Trail.
1.3 Switchbacks.
2.9 Turnaround point.

The hike: From the parking area at the ranger station, cross the road and access the Eldorado Canyon Trailhead. Begin a steep climb up into North Draw. Much work has been done on the lower section of the trail to eliminate cutting switchbacks, so stay on the main trail. You gain altitude quickly as the

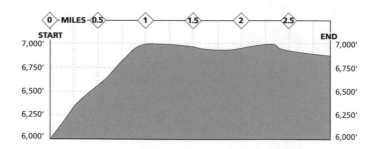

Eldorado Canyon Trail

South Boulder Peak
8,549 ft.

Walker Ranch

North Draw

Eldorado Canyon Trail

Shirt Tail Peak
7,240 ft.

ELDORADO CANYON
STATE PARK

Rattlesnake
Gulch
Trail

START/END

P

F

Fowler Trail

South Boulder Creek

Pay Station

Eldorado Springs

170

N

Kilometer
0   1

Mile
0   1

trail climbs up into North Draw. Great views to the north of Shirt Tail Peak and towering rock walls that are popular with rock climbers from around the world. Eldorado Canyon has been a popular spot for rock climbers since the 1950s and has been at the forefront of Colorado rock climbing since then. At around the 0.4-mile mark the trail climbs past a series of steep switchbacks across a steep hillside. At the top of the switchbacks a climbers' trail on the right leads to the Ricon Wall. You continue straight on the Eldorado Canyon Trail. The trail becomes level and views open to the west to the Indian Peaks and the Continental Divide. Cacti, yuccas, and other sun-loving plants grow on the west-facing hillside that becomes quite colorful with blooming flowers and cacti during the late spring and early summer months. At around the 1.3-mile mark the trail climbs past five steep switchbacks and enters into a dense pine forest. Large, colorful boulders line the trail and a small spring seeps out from one of the boulders just to the right of the trail. The trail curves to the west and crosses over a small seasonal drainage via a wood footbridge. Past the footbridge the trail begin a modest climb up through the pines to an open meadow filled with yuccas and small ponderosas with great views to the east, south, and west. South Boulder Peak (8,549 feet) looms high above to the northeast and the trail cuts a straight line across the meadow and climb up a short, rocky section, gaining a small ridge and high point with great views south to Eldorado Mountain. At around the 2.9-mile mark the trail begins to drop and goes right down into Walker Ranch Open Space (hike #29). This is the turnaround point of this hike. Feel free to drop down to Walker Ranch and South Boulder Creek for more mileage and views.

Denver,
Foothills and
MOUNTAINS

35 Barr Lake State Park

Highlights: *A beautiful, easy hike along the shoreline of Barr Lake, with great views of the Indian Peaks and Rocky Mountain National Park. You can see for a hundred miles to the north and south along the Front Range. This hike offers a different experience than most hikes along the Front Range and is a welcome relief from the steep trails along the foothills and the mountains. This is one of the best spots along the Front Range for wildlife viewing, and there are several spots along the trail where you can stop and look for the many species of birds and mammals that call this special place home. This is a great hike for the whole family to get out and enjoy some excellent hiking in a wonderful wildlife area.*

Season: Year-round.
Distance: 9.2-mile loop.
Difficulty: Easy.
Maps: Barr Lake State Park.

Management: Colorado State Parks.
Trail conditions: The hike follows a smooth doubletrack trail.

Finding the trailhead: From Denver travel north on Interstate 76 to Bromley Lane (exit 22). Go right on Bromley for 1.0 mile to Picadilly Road, then go right on Picadilly Road for 1.7 miles to the park entrance. The hike starts at the Nature Center.

Key points:
1.4 Gazebo Trail.
2.9 Eagle's nest.
4.9 Railroad tracks.
5.8 Dam.
7.9 Boat ramp and picnic area.
9.2 Back at the trailhead.

Barr Lake State Park

Picadilly Road

Park Entrance

N

Kilometer

Mile

waterfowl
hunting area

canal

ditch

canal

canal

dam

Barr Lake

Niedrach Nature Trail

boardwalk

Nature Center

P

START/END

Denver & Hudson Canal

Gazebo Trail

gazebo boardwalk

Barr Lake
Village

76

Oman Canal

The hike: From the Nature Center travel over the Denver and Hudson Canal via a footbridge. Go left, with the canal on your left and the lake on the right. Follow the Niedrach Nature Trail on the right toward the lake. The trail will access the shoreline of the lake via a boardwalk. Large cottonwoods stand near the lake and offer welcome shade during the summer months. The nature trail soon rejoins the main trail and heads west, with great views of the Front Range. Several observation stations are situated in small meadows and can be accessed via side trails; they provide a great opportunity to view the wildlife near the lake.

At the 1.4-mile mark the Gazebo Trail shoots off to the right to a large observation deck. Take the trail if you like. A telescope can be used to sight the many migratory birds that call this area home. Bald eagles nest in the winter months at Barr Lake and can be seen in the large cottonwoods along the shore. Beautiful meadows and cattail marshes line the lake past the Gazebo Trail and offer a different beauty not usually seen along the Front Range.

At around the 2.5-mile mark the trail pulls away from the canal and heads north to the eagle nesting area. At the 2.9-mile mark on the side of the trail is a makeshift tube/pipe that allows a look into an eagle's nest. Take a few minutes to locate the large nest high above the lake in a large cottonwood. Keep an eye out for these beautiful birds during the winter months. Most hikers turn around at this point and retrace their route back to the Nature Center. Feel free to do so, but the rest of the trail is worth the effort to complete the loop.

At around the 4.9-mile mark the trail parallels the railroad tracks for a short distance. Noise from the nearby interstate is quite a contrast to the solitude of the previous miles. Before long the trail meets the north end of the dam and follows a service road past several hunting blinds off to the left in the open fields. This area is popular with hunters during the fall months, so use caution when traveling through this area. At around the 7.8-mile mark the trail follows the canal to the boat ramp access and picnic area. Cross over the road and head south back to the trailhead. Bring a pair of binoculars, water, and a snack and enjoy this beautiful riparian area.

36 Golden Gate State Park

Highlights: *A beautiful and seldom-visited state park located 25 miles west of Denver. The main attractions on this hike are great vistas, wildflowers, colorful aspens in the fall, an old homestead, fishing, and rugged hiking if you do the loop.*

Season: Year-round.
Distance: 8.2-mile loop.
Difficulty: Moderate to difficulty.

Map: Golden Gate State Park.
Management: Colorado State Parks.

Finding the trailhead: From the intersection of U.S. Highway 6 and Colorado Highway 93 near Golden, drive 1.4 miles north on CO 93 and turn left on Golden Gate Canyon Road. Go 12.3 miles to the visitor center and entrance to Golden Gate State Park ($4.00 admission fee). Turn right on Ralston Creek Road and go 1.9 miles to the Bridge Creek Trailhead and a parking lot.

Key points:
0.6 Go left on the Mountain Lion Trail.
1.5 Junction with the Buffalo Trail.
2.5 Junction with the Burro Trail.
4.7 Junction with Quarry Trail.
5.4 Nott Creek Trailhead.
5.9 Eagle Trail.
7.7 Burro Trail.
8.2 Back at the parking area.

The hike: From the trailhead go left up the Burro Trail, climbing steeply to a ridge. At the 0.6-mile mark go left on the Mountain Lion Trail and begin a gradual descent into Forgotten Valley. Forgotten Valley has a pond and old settlement on the left. The pond is stocked with fish, so feel free to drop a line if you brought a rod. If you have the family along this is a great destination in itself and a great spot to bring the kids. Pack a picnic lunch and hang around the pond for pure family fun. For the hard-core hikers this hike is a great loop around the park, with lots of steep and rocky hiking. If you are not up to the task at hand, this is a great spot to turn around and head back to the trailhead.

At around the 1.5-mile mark the hike arrives at a junction with the Buffalo Trail. Continue straight on the Mountain Lion Trail and begin a steep climb up

Golden Gate State Park

N

Kilometer
Mile

Deer Creek

Quarry Trail

quarry

Mountain Lion Trail

Nott Creek Trailhead

Nott Creek

Ralston Creek

Eagle Trail

Mountain Lion Trail

Burro Trail

Burro Trail

Burro Trail

Windy Peak
9,141 ft.

Mountain Lion Trail

City Lights Ridge

Burro Trail

Bridge Creek Trailhead

P START/END

Buffalo Trail

Ralston Creek Road

several switchbacks, heading toward Windy Peak (9,141 feet). At around the 2.3-mile mark you arrive at a notch with great views back to the east. Travel through a dense pine forest and come to a junction with the Burro Trail. Go left on the Mountain Lion Trail and drop down several rocky switchbacks to Deer Creek. Time to get your feet wet; for the next 2 miles the trail crosses Deer Creek several times. During the summer months wildflowers grow profusely in the moist soil along the creek. Old tree bridges help with negotiating the wet terrain, but I found keeping my feet dry almost impossible. Aspens and pine trees cling to the steep hillsides flanking the creek, and in the fall the golden aspens light up the dark, narrow hillsides. The trail breaks out into an open meadow at around the 4.5-mile mark and you quickly arrive at the junction with the Quarry Trail. Go right on the Mountain Lion Trail, crossing a bridge and climbing gently to a trail junction. At the 5.4-mile mark go right and down to the Nott Creek Trailhead and restrooms. Go right at the restrooms and access the Eagle Trail. The Eagle Trail drops down, then climbs steeply up several switchbacks, then drops again to the Burro Trail. Reach a trail junction and then go left on the Burro Trail back to the trailhead and your car.

The history of Golden Gate State Park is almost as colorful as the changing aspens. John Frazer homesteaded in what is now the park and was known to be somewhat of an eccentric. Anders Tallman, a Swedish immigrant, settled what is now Forgotten Valley. He chose this area for its natural beauty and a resemblance to his native homeland. The farmers in the area also made bootleg whisky at harvest time. As many as seventeen stills were in operation during the early 1900s, and the farmers would make daily runs to Denver and Central City to make sure the folks in these early Western towns enjoyed the fruits of their harvest.

37

Mount Galbraith

Highlights: *A beautiful hike up and around Mount Galbraith (7,163 feet) on a new trail in a new Jefferson County Open Space park. There are beautiful vistas in all directions. Wildflowers, yuccas, cacti, cedar, ponderosas, juniper, and lodgepole pines line the trail, which travels through several deep-cut gulches up to Mount Galbraith.*

Season: Year-round.
Distance: 4.0-mile loop.
Difficulty: Moderate.

Maps: Jefferson County Open Space/Mount Galbraith.
Management: Jefferson County Open Space.
Trail conditions: Rocky in sections.

Finding the trailhead: From Denver travel west on U.S. Highway 6 to Golden and Colorado Highway 93. Turn right on CO 93 and travel 2.0 miles to Golden Gate Canyon Road. Turn left on Golden Gate Canyon Road and travel 1.3 miles to the Mount Galbraith Trailhead and parking area on the left.

Key Points:
0.5 Saddle and overlook.
1.3 Junction with the Mount Galbraith Loop Trail.
1.6 Rock steps.
2.1 Overlook.
2.3 Overlook.
2.7 Back at the Cedar Gulch Trail.
4.0 Back at the trailhead.

The hike: From the parking area access the Cedar Gulch Trail near the kiosk and cross over a small seasonal creek. The trail heads west along the creek and begins to climb along the north side of a steep hill. It then cuts across the hillside and passes by a rock wall on the right at the 0.3 mile mark. Beautiful cedar trees cling to the steep hillside along with yuccas and mahogany oak. Reach a small rocky saddle at the 0.5-mile mark, with great views to the east. At the saddle look to the right of the trail and along the ground at all the quartz rocks. You are standing on a barely exposed rock dike. The trail makes a sharp right at the saddle and cuts across the east side of a steep hill. Cedar, juniper, and ponderosa trees lined the trail, along with yuccas and sun-loving prickly-pear cacti. Climb at a steady grade and reach a junction with the Mount Galbraith

Mount Galbraith

To Boulder

To Golden

93

Golden Gate Canyon Road

START/END

P

Cedar Gulch Trail

Mount Galbraith Loop Trail

Mount Galbraith
7,163 ft.

N

Kilometer

Mile

Loop Trail at the 1.3-mile mark. Turn right on the Mount Galbraith Loop Trail and climb across an open steep hill with good views to the east, to a saddle. Reach the saddle and enjoy open views to the north and west. The trail goes left and climbs up a series of rock steps, entering a beautiful stand of ponderosas and lodgepole pines. It is narrow and rocky, with steep dropoffs to the right. It follows a line through the rocks and climbs to an open meadow with expansive views south to Lookout Mountain and west to Mount Evans and the Continental Divide. The meadow is filled with beautiful tall grasses and ponderosas and is a great place to stop and enjoy the views. Follow rock cairns through a rocky area and reach the halfway and high point of the hike. Indian Gulch, Clear Creek, and Clear Creek Canyon are to the south and a thousand feet below you. The trail drops at a gentle grade and cuts through a rocky section, with an overlook on the right. Head to the north and reach a second overlook in a small, open meadow, with stunted ponderosas along both sides of the trail. Enjoy great views and follow the trail along the east side of Mount Galbraith and back to the Cedar Gulch Trail. Turn right on the Cedar Gulch Trail, enjoying open views to the east and north, and retrace your route back to the trailhead.

38

Chimney Gulch

Highlights: *A steep hike into and up Chimney Gulch, located a mile from downtown Golden. Excellent views of Denver, the plains, and up Clear Creek Canyon from Wind Saddle. The trail climbs through Chimney Gulch and along steep hillsides covered with wildflowers, cacti, yuccas, and mixed pine forests. This is a year-round trail that is especially beautiful during the early summer months.*

Season: Year-round.
Distance: 3.5 miles one way.
Difficulty: Moderate.
Maps: Jefferson County Open Space/Lookout Mountain.

Management: Jefferson County Open Space.
Trail conditions: Smooth on the lower section and quite rocky above Windy Saddle.

Finding the trailhead: From Denver travel west on U.S. Highway 6 to Colorado Highway 93 in Golden. Travel south on Colorado 93 for 0.5 mile to a parking area on the right. The parking area is located just past a large TOWN OF GOLDEN sign and at a windsock (used by paragliders). The hike starts here.

Key points:
0.7 Private driveway.
0.9 Lookout Mountain Road.
1.8 Wood bridge.
2.2 Second wood bridge.
2.41 Lookout Mountain Road and Windy Saddle.
2.6 Junction with Beaver Brook Trail.
3.5 Colorow Road and Lookout Mountain Nature Center.

The hike: From the parking area follow the narrow trail north across a small, open meadow. Watch out for landing paragliders. When you reach a dirt road, go left up the road to a cement ditch. Walk over the ditch and head right and up a narrow trail with beautiful yuccas along both sides. Follow the trail through a short, rocky section to the crest of a small hill and a trail junction. Go left (southwest) up the narrow trail and into Chimney Gulch. The trail hugs the side of the gulch, with nice-looking cottonwoods to the left. Follow a series of steep switchbacks up to a private driveway. At the driveway turn left, following the trail markers. Make a quick right onto a narrow trail, passing a house on the left, and climb to Lookout Mountain Road. After 0.9 mile of fairly steep hiking you arrive at Lookout Mountain Road. Cross Lookout Mountain

Chimney Gulch

To Boulder

93

58

Clear Creek

Golden

START/END

P

6

Mount
Zion

Gulch

Lookout
Mountain Rd.

6

Beaver Brook Trail

Chimney

Windy
Saddle

Windy Saddle Park

Lookout
Mountain
Trail

To Denver

Lookout
Mountain
Nature
Center

Colorow Road

Lookout
Mountain

N

0   Kilometer   1

0   Mile   1

To 40 70

Road to the trail on the other side. Watch out for car traffic. Follow the trail up and into Chimney Gulch past several rocky sections. This section of the trail hugs the north side of the gulch and is filled with blooming wildflowers and yuccas during the early summer months. At around the 1.6-mile mark the trail becomes quite narrow, passing through a stand of young cottonwood trees. The trail follows the contour of the steep hill and stays close to a seasonal creek down and to the left. Arrive at a wood footbridge where the trail cuts sharply back to the east. There are views here of Golden, Table Mountain, Denver, tract houses, and the sprawling Coors Brewery. The trail climbs through a beautiful forest of juniper, Douglas firs, and ponderosa pines. Reach a second footbridge and climb to the north away from Chimney Gulch to Lookout Mountain Road at the 2.4-mile mark. This is a good spot to take a short rest and enjoy the views east to Denver and west up Clear Creek Canyon. Go left up Lookout Mountain Road to the Lookout Mountain/Beaver Brook Trails on the right. Follow these trails up into the pines, with excellent views to the west, where the trails split at the 2.6-mile mark. The Beaver Brook Trail heads north (right) and the Lookout Mountain Trail goes left (west). Follow the Lookout Mountain Trail up through a shady area of tall pines to an overlook at the 2.9-mile mark. Stop at the lookout and enjoy views to the west. The trail climbs up through the pines at a gentle grade and reaches Colorow Road and the Lookout Mountain Nature Center at the 3.5-mile mark. This is the turn-around point for this hike.

Feel free to visit the Lookout Mountain Nature Center, located near the Boettcher Mansion. The nature center is a great place to bring the family and learn about the ecology, geology, and animal life in the area. The center runs year-round programs and is open everyday except Monday from 10:00 A.M. to 4:00 P.M. Call (303) 526–0594 for more information.

39

Apex Park

Highlights: *Situated below Lookout Mountain, and surrounded by the ever-increasing urban sprawl, lies this beautiful piece of open space. Apex Park is a quick getaway into a beautiful deep gulch that offers hikers great views, beautiful wildflowers, cacti, yuccas, and a pine forest, a mere 15 miles from downtown Denver.*

Season: Year-round.
Distance: 5.3-mile loop.
Difficulty: Moderate.
Maps: Jefferson County Open Space/ Reynolds Park.

Management: Jefferson County Open Space.
Trail conditions: Rocky in sections.

Finding the trailhead: From Denver go west on Interstate 70 to the Morrison exit (U.S. Highway 40). Go 1.0 mile east on US 40 to just past the Heritage Square entrance and make a left. Make another quick left into the Apex Park east parking lot just before Golden Fire Station No. 4.

Key points:
0.7 Pick 'n' Sledge Trail.
1.4 Sluice Box Trail.
1.9 Bonanza Trail and Grubstake Trail junction.
4.6 Back at the Apex Trail.
5.3 Back at the trailhead.

The hike: Once the site of the thriving town of Apex and a toll road to the gold mines of Central City and Blackhawk, Apex Open Space Park is a beautiful oasis in an area of ever-increasing urban sprawl. From the parking area head west along a seasonal creek and nice cottonwoods. Cross over a bridge and follow the wide trail through a large lot up to the start of the gulch and a

Apex Park

To Denver

40

To 70

70

Heritage Road

To Golden

START/END

P

Heritage Square

Apex Trail

Sledge Trail

Pick

Grubstake Trail

Bonanza Trail

Grubstake Trail

Apex Trail

Sluice Box Trail

Lookout Mountain Road

N

Kilometer

Mile

0 1

0 1

toll road sign. The trail you are now traveling on was once used by miners and supply wagons going to and from the gold mines near Blackhawk and Central City. Follow the trail into the gulch along the creek. The trail becomes somewhat rocky and climbs to a junction with Pick 'n' Sledge Trail. Wildflowers, scrub oak, cacti, and yuccas grow along with the occasional cottonwood through this section of the gulch. Continue west up the gulch to the Sluicebox Trail at the 1.4-mile mark. Go right on the Sluicebox Trail and climb eleven switchbacks to a junction with the Bonanza and Grubstake Trails. Continue straight on the Grubstake Trail and enter a forest of lodgepole and ponderosa pines. Pleasant hiking through the pines takes you through an open meadow and along the east side of Indian Mountain. Enjoy views to the north and east while traversing the eastside of Indian Mountain. The trail takes a steep drop down an open hillside to the Apex Trail. The hill is covered in yuccas and cacti and uses three steep switchbacks to reach the Apex Trail and the creek. Go left on the Apex Trail and retrace your route back to the trailhead.

Beaver Brook Trail

Highlights: *A nice hike in the trees high above Clear Creek and Clear Creek Canyon. The Beaver Brook Trail runs in an east-to-west direction for 7 miles. Feel free to extend your mileage and hike as far as you like. Beautiful views up and down Clear Creek Canyon and west to the Continental Divide.*

Season: Year-round.
Distance: 1.6 miles one way.
Difficulty: Easy to moderate.
Maps: Denver Mountain Parks/Beaver Brook Trail.

Management: Denver Mountain Parks.
Trail conditions: The trail is extremely rocky in sections.

Finding the trailhead: From Denver travel west on U.S. Highway 6 to Golden. Travel south on Colorado Highway 93 for 1.5 miles to Lookout Mountain Road. Travel 4.4 miles on Lookout Mountain Road to Windy Saddle, the trailhead, and parking.

Beaver Brook Trail

To Golden

Windy Saddle Park

Lookout Mountain Road

Windy Saddle

To Lookout Mountain

START/END

Lookout Mountain Trail

Colrow Road

Lookout Mountain Nature Center

Clear Creek

6

Canyon

Clear Creek

Beaver Brook Trail

Beaver Brook

Turnaround point

N

Kilometer

Mile

Key points:

0.1 Junction with the Lookout Mountain Trail.
0.7 Seasonal stream crossing.
1.6 Open meadow and turnaround point.

The hike: From the parking area at Windy Saddle pass the kiosk and access the Lookout Mountain Trail. Follow the Lookout Mountain Trail into the trees and up to a junction with Beaver Brook Trail. At the junction travel right on the Beaver Brook Trail. Follow the trail into the trees and reach a cluster of boulders on the trail. Stay to the left and uphill side of the boulders. The trail cuts through two large boulders, then rolls to a series of rocky sections. Scramble through the boulders and reach a narrow gully with a seasonal stream. A tall rock cliff looms above the trail, and the steep slope drops to Clear Creek on the right. Continue on the narrow path and cut across a slide area. The trail begins to descend into the woods, passing several rocky sections, and enters an open area filled with tall grasses and views to the east, down to Clear Creek and U.S. Highway 6. At around the 1.3-mile mark the trail crosses a seasonal stream and travels through a dense pine forest to an open meadow. Right of the trail is a flat, rocky ledge that offers great views of Clear Creek Canyon. Continue on if you have the time; this hike ends here. Retrace your route back to Windy Saddle.

41 Dakota Ridge Trail

Highlights: *A trip back into time. Dinosaurs once roamed this land millions of years ago, and this hike takes you to the fossilized remains and footprints of these prehistoric animals via the Dakota Ridge Trail and Rooney Road.*

Season: Year-round.
Distance: 2.1 miles one way.
Difficulty: Easy to moderate.
Maps: Jefferson County Open Space/ Matthews-Winters Open Space Park.

Management: Jefferson County Open Space.
Trail conditions: The trail is rocky.

Finding the trailhead: From Denver travel west on Interstate 70 to the Morrison/Golden exit and Colorado Highway 26. Travel west on CO 26 for 0.2 mile to the Matthews/Winters Open Space parking area on the right. Turn right into the parking. The hike starts here.

Key points:
0.8 The trail goes right.
2.1 Alameda Parkway.

The hike: From the parking area cross CO 26 and access the fire road on the east side of the highway. Pass through a gate and climb up to a trail marker at the 0.8-mile mark. Go right at the trail marker and climb along the crest of the ridge. The Dakota Ridge Trail cuts through a forest of small juniper and ponderosa pines and stays on the west side of the ridge. Reach a trail marker and the top of the ridge. The trail cuts to the east side of the ridge and drops on rocky tread into a small meadow. Wildflowers, cacti, and yuccas bloom in the late spring along with meadow grass in this picturesque little meadow. Follow the trail through the meadow and climb past several wood steps through the pines to reach a high point on the ridge. The trail is extremely rocky through this section. Great views open to the east to Green Mountain and Denver, west to Mount Morrison, and south to Pikes Peak towering in the southern skyline. The trail climbs a short distance and passes several sandstone outcrops on the right, coming extremely close to the edge of one of the cliffs. It then cuts to the left and drops steeply past several waterbars to a trail junction. Go left at the junction, switchbacking on rocky tread down to Rooney Road. Go left on Rooney Road past several interpretive signs on the left to a large kiosk and dinosaur tracks. After exploring this area hike back up Rooney

Dakota Ridge Trail

Road past the Dakota Ridge Trail and read the interpretive signs along Rooney Road to the west. After enjoying your dinosaur tour, retrace your route back on the Dakota Ridge Trail to the trailhead. This trail is extremely popular with hikers and mountain cyclists on weekends. Watch out for other trail users.

42 Matthews/Winters Open Space

Highlights: *A beautiful hike up and through the foothills of Matthews/Winters Open Space Park. This hike takes you past the old cemetery and townsite of Mt. Vernon, through open meadows filled with wildflowers with spectacular views to the north, east to Green Mountain and Dakota Ridge, and south to Pikes Peak.*

Season: Year-round.
Distance: 5.0-mile loop.
Difficulty: Easy to moderate
Maps: Jefferson County Open Space/
Matthews-Winters Open Space Park.

Management: Jefferson County Open Space.
Trail conditions: The trail is rocky.

Finding the trailhead: From Denver travel west on Interstate 70 to the Morrison/Golden exit and Colorado Highway 26. Travel west on CO 26 for 0.2 mile to the Matthews/Winters Open Space parking area on the right. Turn right into the parking. The hike starts here.

Key points:
    0.4 Mt. Vernon townsite and cemetery and Red Rocks Trail.
    1.2 Morrison Slide Trail.
    2. 7 Red Rocks Trail.
    4.3 Village Walk Trail.
    5.0 Back at the parking area.

Matthews/Winters Open Space

To Denver

To Denver

40

70

40 70

Mount Vernon Creek

START/END 🅿 🚶

Village Walk Trail

Mount Vernon
Townsite and
Cemetery

Dakota Ridge Trail

26

To Alameda
Parkway

Red Rocks Trail

Rooney Road

Morrison Slide Trail

Red Rocks Trail

Mount
▲ Morrison
7,886 ft.

Dinosaur
tracks

Red Rocks Trail

N

Red Rocks Park
and Amphitheatre

To Morrison

0   Kilometer   1

0   Mile   1

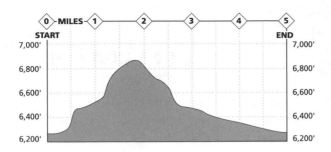

The hike: From the parking area go down the steps and pick up a park map at the kiosk. Follow the wide gravel path down past the restrooms and picnic area to a bridge. Cross the wood footbridge over Mt. Vernon Creek and follow the Village Walk Trail up and to the right. Mt. Vernon Creek is quite picturesque and is surrounded by tall cottonwoods and willow bushes. The Village Walk Trail climbs up a gentle grade through an open meadow filled with colorful wildflowers in the late spring and early summer months. The trail makes a sharp left at the top of the hill and climbs up to the Mt. Vernon townsite. Reach the townsite (not much left), cemetery, and a junction with the Red Rocks Trail. Check out the cemetery, then turn right on the Red Rocks Trail, following this beautiful trail in and out of several gulches and over two creek crossings to a junction with the Morrison Slide Trail. Go up and to the right on the Morrison Slide Trail and climb steeply, passing several switchbacks with excellent views to the north and east. The trail slices its way through the boulder-strewn hillside and makes a narrow passage through two large boulders to reach an overlook at the 1.8-mile mark. This is a good spot to take a break and enjoy the awesome views. Follow the trail up through a large open meadow, filled with prairie grasses, wildflowers, yuccas, and widely spaced juniper trees. Enjoy excellent views to the east and south. The trail hugs the edge of the meadow, with steep dropoffs to the left. At the 2.3-mile mark the trail makes a steep drop down several rocky switchbacks, with beautiful views to the south and towering red rock formations. Reach the Red Rocks Trail again at the 2.7-mile mark and climb several wood steps to the crest of a hill and great views. The trail heads back to the north, clinging to the side of a steep hill through the juniper trees and meets the Morrison Slide Trail at the 3.5-mile mark. Drop down, crossing a familiar creek, and follow the Red Rocks Trail back toward the Mt. Vernon townsite. Enjoy hiking with good views to the north and reach the Village Walk Trail at the 4.3-mile mark. Turn right on the Village Walk Trail and descend, passing rocks, trees, and tall shrubs to reach Mt. Vernon Creek. Follow the trail along the creek under the canopy of tall cottonwoods and reach the footbridge. Go right across the footbridge past the restrooms and picnic area and reach the end of the hike and the parking area.

43   Mount Falcon Open Space

Highlights: *A nice hike with spectacular views of Red Rocks, the Continental Divide, and the plains. Expect to see wildlife, wildflowers, cacti, beautiful yuccas, and great views to the north, east, and west.*

Season: Year-round.
Distance: 9.5-mile loop.
Difficulty: Moderate to strenuous.
Maps: Jefferson County Open Space/Mount Falcon Park.

Management: Jefferson County Open Space.
Trail conditions: The trail on the lower part of the hike is rocky in sections. The Parmalee Trail is rocky.

Finding the trailhead: From Denver travel west on Interstate 70 to the Morrison/Golden exit and Colorado Highway 26. Travel west on CO 26 for 4.0 miles to the town of Morrison. Go right on Main Street in Morrison and then go left on Colorado Highway 8 for 1.6 miles to Forest Avenue. Turn right on Forest Avenue and follow the signs for Mount Falcon Open Space, the trailhead, and the parking area.

Key Points:
0.7 Views north to Red Rocks.
2.7 Junction with the Two-Dog Trail.
3.7 Junction with the Parmalee Trail.
6.0 Junction with the Meadow Trail.
6.4 Back at the Castle Trail.
9.5 Back at the trailhead.

The hike: From the parking area drop down on the Castle Trail across a small gulch. Begin a steep climb through junipers, cacti, and yuccas, with good views to the east. At around the 0.7-mile mark the trail switchbacks to the north, with great views of Red Rocks. The trail turns back to the south and climbs several switchbacks. At around the 1.7-mile mark great views of Morrison and Denver appear. This is a good spot to take a short break. The trail climbs into the pines and becomes quite steep and rocky at the 2.3-mile mark. Power forward and within a short distance reach a saddle and trail junction. The trail to the right leads to the Summer White House ruins and is 0.4-mile long. The trail going to the left is the Two-Dog Trail, which leads to an overlook and is 0.2-mile long. For this hike we continue on the Castle Trail, climbing at a gentle grade to a junction with the Meadow Trail at the 3.4-mile mark.

Mount Falcon Open Space

Wildflowers bloom in the early summer months along this section of the trail. Stay to the right on the Castle Trail, dropping down a short hill and passing the Walker Home ruins on the right. At around the 3.7-mile mark, pass the restrooms on the right and make a quick left to the Parmalee Trail. The Parmalee Trail is 2.0-miles long, quite narrow, and crosses several seasonal creeks. It travels through ponderosas pines and hovers high above U.S. Highway 285, offering great views to the south and east. The trail can be quite rocky in sections and extremely narrow. Watch out for others trail users and yield the right-of-way to the uphill traveler. At around the 6.0-mile mark reach a junction with the Meadow Trail. Go right on the Meadow Trail and then make a quick left onto the Meadow Trail at a junction with the Old Ute Trail. Follow the Meadow Trail across an open area. Reach the Castle Trail at the 6.4-mile mark and get ready for some fast downhill hiking. Go right on the Castle Trail and retrace your route back to the parking area. Feel free to make this hike as long or short as you as you desire. Pick up a map at the trailhead and customize a hike to fit your time frame and ability.

44 Deer Creek Canyon Park

Highlights: *A nice hike through the beautiful foothills west of Denver. Year-round access, marked trails, early summer wildflowers, and spectacular views from the summit of Plymouth Mountain (7,295 feet).*

Season: Year-round.
Distance: 2.8 miles one way.
Difficulty: Moderate.
Maps: Jefferson County Open Space/Deer Creek Canyon Park.

Management: Jefferson County Open Space.
Trail conditions: Smooth on the lower section, rocky near the summit of Plymouth Mountain.

Finding the trailhead: From Denver travel west on Interstate 70 to Highway C–470 east. Travel east on C–470 to the Wadsworth Boulevard exit (Colorado Highway 121). Exit onto Wadsworth Boulevard and go south for 300 yards to Deer Creek Canyon Road. Turn west on Deer Creek Canyon Road and travel 4.9 miles to the park entrance. The hike starts near the restrooms.

Key points:
1.9 Plymouth Mountain Trail.
2.4 Junction with the Scenic View Trail.
2.8 Summit of Plymouth Mountain.

The hike: From the parking area access the well-marked Plymouth Creek Trail. Follow the Plymouth Creek Trail south on smooth tread. The trail stays level for a short distance then begins a steady climb into the pines trees, with Plymouth Creek on your left. Be on the lookout for wildflowers that bloom in the early summer months along the banks and hillsides of the creek. The trail becomes rough and rocky as you climb to a junction with the Meadowlark Trail on the right. Continue straight on the Plymouth Creek Trail and grind

Deer Creek Canyon Park

your way through a steep, rocky section of the trail. Slow things down a bit, catch your breath, and enjoy the beautiful hiking along Plymouth Creek. At around the 1.9-mile mark reach a junction with the Plymouth Mountain Trail. Turn left and follow the Plymouth Mountain Trail into the pines. Look east for excellent views of Denver and the plains. Climb at a steady rate and reach a junction with the Scenic View Trail on the left. This is a nice spot to take a break. Go left on the Scenic View Trail as it curves to the north and climbs steadily to the summit of Plymouth Mountain. There are excellent views to the north and east as you reach the summit at the 2.8-mile mark. Take a short break and enjoy the wonderful views before retracing your route back to the parking area.

Reynolds Park Open Space

Highlights: *Tucked away in Kennedy Gulch is this prime piece of open space about 6 miles south of the town of Conifer. As in other open space areas in Jefferson County, the trails are maintained and marked. A stiff climb to the Eagle's View Trail leads to a spectacular overlook of the South Platte area and panoramic views to the east, west, and south.*

Season: Year-round.
Distance: 4.1-mile loop.
Difficulty: Moderate.
Maps: Jefferson County Open Space/ Reynolds Park

Management: Jefferson County Open Space.
Trail conditions: Rocky in sections.

Finding the trailhead: From Denver travel south on U.S. Highway 285 to the town of Conifer. Travel through Conifer to Foxton Road. Go left on Foxton Road for 5.2 miles to Reynolds Open Space and a parking area on the right.

Key points:
0.4 Raven's Roost Trail.
1.0 Trail junction.
1.3 Trail junction.
2.0 Overlook.
2.7 Oxen Draw Trail.
3.3 Elkhorn Trail.

Reynolds Park Open Space

3.5 Songbird Trail.
4.0 Foxton Road.
4.1 Back at the parking area.

The hike: From the parking area go right past the restrooms to the Elkhorn Trail. Go right on the Elkhorn Trail and begin a steep climb past several switchbacks toward the Raven's Roost Trail. Yuccas, cacti, and wildflowers grow on this open south-facing slope. At around the 0.4-mile mark go left on the Raven's Roost Trail and continue climbing into a forest of tall spruce trees up to where the Raven's Roost Trail goes to the left and drops down to a small creek crossing. At around the 1.3-mile mark you arrive at a junction with the Eagle View and Oxen Draw Trails. Go right on the Eagle View Trail and climb steadily through the trees to a ridgeline and a small, open meadow. Arrive at the overlook where the trail ends near an old fire pit. Enjoy the spectacular views to the east, south, and west. Looking west you can easily identify the large burn area left by the fire of 1996 that charred more than 12,000 acres of prime Pike National Forest land. Take a few minutes to enjoy the views, then head back down the Eagle View Trail to the Oxen Draw Trail. Go right on the Oxen Draw Trail and cross the stream several times. Negotiate a few rocky sections, and at the 3.3-mile mark arrive at the Elkhorn Trail. The Elkhorn Trail is 0.9-mile long and has several interpretive signs that explain local fauna and geology. Feel free to take this side trail to enhance your visit to Reynolds Park. Then follow the Elkhorn Trail for 0.2 mile to the Songbird Trail. Go right on the Songbird Trail and cruise along the stream on a slight downhill grade. Be on the lookout for wildflowers that grow in the late spring and early summer months along the stream. At the 3.9-mile mark travel over a small wood bridge. Cross the bridge where the trail dumps you at the lower parking area. Go left up Foxton Road to the upper parking area and your car.

Option: At the 4.0-mile mark cross Foxton Road and take the Hummingbird Trail up the north side of Kennedy Gulch and loop back to the upper parking, adding 1.3 miles to your hike.

46

Elk Meadow Park

Highlights: *A rolling, beautiful hike in Elk Meadow Park Wildlife Preserve. On this hike expect to see early season wildflowers, western meadowlarks, prairie grasses, mule deer, ponderosas, tall Douglas firs, and if you're lucky bugling elk.*

Season: Year-round.
Distance: 5.4-mile loop.
Difficulty: Easy to moderate.
Maps: Jefferson County Open Space/Deer Creek Canyon Park.

Management: Jefferson County Open Space.
Trail conditions: The trail for the most part is fairly smooth.

Finding the trailhead: From Denver travel west on Interstate 70 to Colorado Highway 74 (Evergreen Parkway). Travel 5.0 miles south on CO 74 to Stagecoach Boulevard. Turn right on Stagecoach Boulevard and travel 1.3 miles to a parking area and trailhead on the right. The hike starts here.

Key points:

0.3 Junction with the Meadow View Trail.
0.9 Junction with the Bergen Peak Trail.
1.1 Junction with the Elkridge Trail.
2.1 Junction with the Too Long Trail.
3.0 Junction with Painters Pause Trail.
4.0 Junction with the Sleepy "S" Trail.
5.4 Back at the trailhead.

The hike: From the parking area head north on the Sleepy "S" Trail. Enjoy level hiking and smooth tread to the junction with the Meadow View Trail. Turn left on the Meadow View Trail and climb through the ponderosas and aspens at a gentle grade to a junction with the Bergen Peak Trail. There are nice views to the north and east to Elk Meadow. At the trail junction with the Bergen Peak Trail (0.9-mile mark), continue straight on the Meadow View Trail. The trail is fairly smooth and rolls along, with an open view of the meadow and to the north and east. Tall grasses grow along with cacti, wildflowers, and pine trees. At the 1.1-mile mark you reach a junction with the Elkridge Trail and views to the east. (Those of you who want to shorten the hike can make a right on the Elkridge Trail; after a 0.5-mile hike you arrive at

Elk Meadow Park

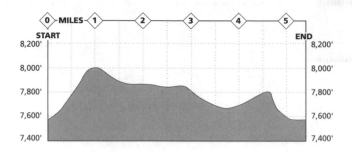

a junction with the Sleepy "S" Trail. Go right on the Sleepy "S" Trail and in less than a mile you are back at the parking area.)

For this hike we continue on the beautiful, rolling Meadow View Trail north, with open views. Be on the lookout for mule deer and other wildlife through this section of the hike. At the 2.1-mile mark you arrive at a junction with the Too Long Trail on the left. This is a nice spot to take a short break. Turn right and continue on the Meadow View Trail, losing elevation and heading to the east and toward CO 74. After almost 2 miles of beautiful hiking, at the 3.0-mile mark, you reach a junction with Painters Pause Trail. Go right on the Painters Pause Trail, with CO 74 on your left. Late spring and early summer is a wonderful time to do this hike. The meadow is filled with green prairie grasses, numerous wildflowers, and the beautiful song of the western meadowlark drowning out the sound of the passing cars and trucks on the highway. Look west to the rocky summit of Bergen Peak (9,708 feet). Roll down the trail and arrive at a junction with the Sleepy "S" Trail at the 4.0-mile mark. Turn right on the Sleepy "S" Trail and climb past several waterbars up into a beautiful meadow. Enjoy beautiful and sometimes steep hiking in a forest of scattered ponderosas. Take a break on a bench just left of the trail. Travel to a junction with the Meadow View Trail. Turn left on the Meadow View Trail and drop back to the trailhead.

47

Bergen Peak

Highlights: *A beautiful hike up to the summit of Bergen Peak (9,708 feet). Expect to see wildlife, wildflowers along the trail, and excellent views from atop the summit. This is an excellent hike and a must-do. It is popular with other trail users, so show common courtesy and say a few kind words to others.*

Season: March to November.
Distance: 4.6 miles one way.
Difficulty: Moderate to strenuous.
Maps: Jefferson County Open Space/Deer Creek Canyon Park.

Management: Jefferson County Open Space.
Trail conditions: The trail is steep and rocky and uses several switchbacks to negotiate the steeper sections.

Finding the trailhead: From Denver travel west on Interstate 70 to Colorado Highway 74 (Evergreen Parkway). Travel 5.0 miles south on CO 74 to Stagecoach Boulevard. Turn right on Stagecoach Boulevard and travel 1.3 miles to a parking area and trailhead on the right. The hike starts here.

Key Points:
0.3 Junction with the Meadow View Trail.
0.9 Junction with the Bergen Peak Trail.
3.6 Junction with the Too Long Trail.
4.6 Summit of Bergen Peak.

The hike: From the parking area head north on the Sleepy "S" Trail. Enjoy level hiking and smooth tread up to a junction with the Meadow View Trail. Turn left on the Meadow View Trail and climb at a gentle grade to a junction with the Bergen Peak Trail. There are nice views to the north and Elk Meadow. Elk Meadow is an important winter grazing area for elk and mule deer. Reach the Bergen Peak Trail at the 0.9-mile mark. Go left on the Bergen Peak Trail and climb past several steep sections. Waterbars and wood steps help to keep erosion in check on the steep part of the trail. Switchback up through the pines and reach another steep section with switchbacks. Power up through this section and reach the top of the switchbacks. Take a break and enjoy great views to the north and south. Follow the Bergen Peak Trail as it curves to the north and drops to a junction with Too Long Trail. Hope you enjoyed that downhill; things get steep from here to the summit of Bergen Peak. Turn left, staying on the Bergen Peak Trail. Grind through a steep, rocky section and climb to an overlook with views to the north, east, and south. Take

Bergen Peak

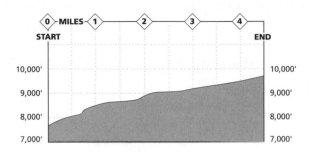

a quick breather and continue to climb past three switchbacks. The trail heads to the west and actually drops a short distance before the last climb to the summit. Views to the west and north make the last steep pitch doable. Follow the steep trail up through a rocky section and reach the summit of Bergen Peak. This is a great spot to relax, eat some lunch, and take in the panoramic views in all directions. Views like this make all that climbing worth it. After taking lots of photographs and a long break, retrace your route back to the trailhead.

This is an extremely popular area with other trail users, and for good reason. Keep in mind that they (mountain cyclists and equestrians) have the same rights and privileges that you do. Thank other trail users when they yield to you. To make your hike of Bergen Peak a quiet and more enjoyable experience, do the hike midweek when there are fewer trail users and a lot more solitude.

Chief Mountain

Highlights: *A short hike up to the rocky summit of Chief Mountain (11,709 feet). The trail gains over 1,100 feet in 1.5 miles, but once on top of Chief Mountain you are rewarded for all that hard work with spectacular views to the north, south, and east to the plains.*

Season: Spring to fall.
Distance: 1.5 miles one way.
Difficulty: Moderate.
Maps: Trails Illustrated Idaho Springs/ Georgetown/Loveland Pass #104.

Management: Arapaho National Forest.
Trail conditions: The trail is fairly smooth on the lower section but becomes quite rocky near the summit.

Finding the trailhead: From Denver take Interstate 70 west to exit 252 (Evergreen Parkway). Follow Evergreen Parkway (Colorado Highway 74) south for just over 2.9 miles to Colorado Highway 103. Go right on CO 103 for 12.1 miles to a pullout on the right side of the road. The hike starts here.

Key points:
0.2 Old Squaw Pass Road.
0.3 Papoose Mountain on the left.
0.9 Open alpine tundra.
1.2 Summit saddle.
1.5 Chief Mountain summit.

The hike: From the pullout cross Squaw Pass Road and pick up a trail that switchbacks up a steep hill. Pass by a cement post marked 290 and climb into the tall spruce trees. Climb through the trees and pass a small kiosk. Arrive at Old Squaw Pass Road at around the 0.2-mile mark. Cross the road to the Chief Mountain Trail. The sign says 2.0 miles to the summit, but by my GPS system it is really only 1.3 miles. Climb to a saddle with Papoose Mountain (11,174 feet) on the left and Chief Mountain looming high above you on the right. The trail now makes a steady climb through the trees on the north side of Chief Mountain, making use of long switchbacks, and quickly gains altitude. At around the 0.9-mile mark the trail breaks out of the trees and enters alpine tundra. Dramatic views open to the west to Mount Evans, north to the Indian Peaks and Longs Peak, and east to the plains. The trail cuts through the open tundra and heads west, passing two switchbacks. Lichen-covered rocks are scattered everywhere, and small alpine flowers grow in the rocky soil. The views are spectacular and the hiking is wonderful through this section of the trail. Reach a huge, flat-top boulder along the side of the trail. Stop here and take in the views. Soon gain the summit saddle and travel through a sparse forest of stunted bristlecone pines and subalpine firs. Panoramic views and colorful rocks surround you as you quickly gain the rock-covered summit. Enjoy the views, take a break, and don't rush to leave this spot. Longs Peak and

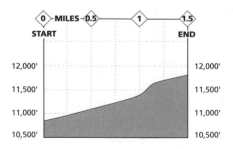

Chief Mountain

N

Kilometer

Mile

0

0

To Bergen Peak

Squaw Pass Road

Old Squaw Pass Road

Papoose Mountain
11,174 ft.

Squaw Pass
Ski Area
Site

START/ END

Chief
Mountain Trail

Chief Mountain
11,709 ft.

103

P

To Mount Evans Road

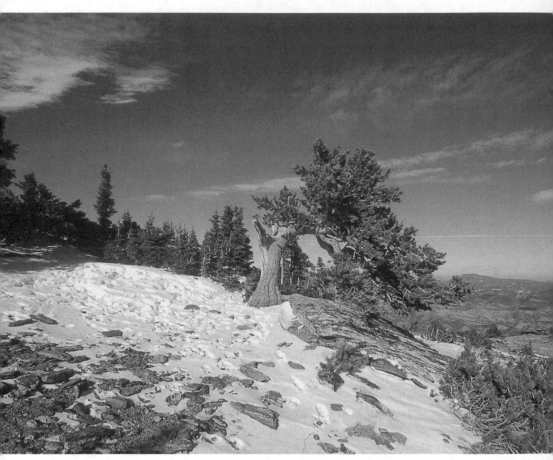

Chief Mountain

Mount Meeker are far to the north, Mount Evans and Mount Bierstadt are to the west, Pikes Peak is to the south, and Denver and the plains are to the east. It's hard to believe that you can have these views on an 11,709-foot summit. Retrace your route back to the trailhead. Once back at your car look down and to the north. Remnants of the old Squaw Pass Ski Area lifts lie dormant on the steep north-facing slope.

49

Mount Bierstadt

Highlights: *Everybody wants to do a "fourteener," and this is one of the most accessible near the Front Range. The trail is well marked and easy to the follow, with little chance of getting off track. The views of the surrounding peaks are spectacular and become more impressive the higher you climb.*

Season: June to October.
Distance: 3.7 miles one way.
Difficulty: Moderate to strenuous.
Maps: Trails Illustrated Idaho Springs/ Georgetown/Loveland Pass #104.

Management: South Platte Ranger District/ USDA Forest Service.
Trail conditions: The trail is well maintained and extremely smooth for the first 2.5 miles. The upper section is rocky and steep.

Finding the trailhead: From Denver follow Interstate 70 west to Georgetown. Travel through Georgetown to Guanella Pass Road. Follow Guanella Pass Road for 10.0 miles to the Mount Bierstadt Trailhead on the left. The hike starts here.

Key points:
0.2 Deadmans Lake.
1.0 Creek crossing.
1.5 Steep climb.
3.3 South saddle.
3.7 The summit.

The hike: From the trailhead the trail drops into the willows toward Deadmans Lake on the left. The trail travels through heavy willows and wet areas on several new wood bridges. Before the bridges were established in this area, the trail was hard to follow and extremely wet. Thanks to the Forest Service and all the volunteers who helped construct the bridges and worked on the trail. There are several tarns in this area, and wildflowers grow profusely in the moist soil. After a mile of easy hiking you cross Scott Gomer Creek. This can be dangerous during early summer runoff, so use caution during times of high runoff. After the stream crossing the trail begins to climb through the willows on smooth tread; enjoyable hiking. Around the 1.5-mile mark the trail climbs steeply to a large, open meadow. Mount Bierstadt (14,060 feet) dominates the skyline in the east with the rocky, jagged summit of the Sawtooth to the left. The steep, rocky walls of the Sawtooth face to the northwest and appear dark and ominous for most of the day, creating an impressive

Mount Bierstadt

Mount Evans Road

Summit Lake

Mount Evans
14,264 ft.

Abyss Lake

Mount Spaulding
13,842 ft.

Greywolf
Mountain
13,602 ft.

The Sawtooth

Mount
Bierstadt
14,060 ft.

Frozen Lake

Scott Gomer Creek

Mount Bierstadt Trail 711

N

Kilometer

Mile

Deadmans
Lake

START/END

Rosalie Trail 603

Guanella Pass
Campground

Guanella
Pass

Guanella Pass Road

South Park Trail 600

Duck Lake

and intimidating alpine cirque. The meadow you are now traveling through is home to the rare Uncompaghre butterfly. This small insect makes its home in the snow willows that grow on tundra in high alpine meadows. Be careful not to go off the trail as the tundra flowers, grasses, and willows are extremely fragile and susceptible to human and animal intrusion. Things get a little more serious from this point on. The trail becomes rockier, with sections of stone steps making the going easier as you climb up to a shelf running south. The lay of the land changes drastically as you gain altitude and shoot back to the north into a large boulder field below the south saddle of Mount Bierstadt. Rock cairns mark the way up through the boulder field and keep you going in the right direction. For some strange reason the summit of Mount Bierstadt, off and up to the left, looks closer than it really is. Don't get discouraged, keep cranking and before you know it you arrive in a somewhat level boulder field along the south saddle. This is a good spot to take a break and enjoy the panoramic views. Ramble over to the saddle and peer down at Frozen Lake, neatly tucked below. If the weather is changing for the worse, this is not the place to be. Summer thunderstorms are extremely dangerous, and exposed ridges are not the places to be hanging out. The trail now goes to the north along the south ridgeline of Mount Bierstadt and into the boulders. Small cairns mark the way along this strenuous section to the summit. After less than a quarter mile of steep hiking, arrive at the summit of Mount Bierstadt and take a well-deserved rest. Looking to the north you can see the summit of Mount Evans (14,264 feet), Abyss Lake, and the paved Mount Evans Road. Turn to the west and the twin fourteeners, Grays (14,270 feet) and Torreys (14,267 feet) Peaks, stand high in the western sky. The views are panoramic, spectacular, and extend in all directions. This is why you climb a fourteener. After your rest, turn around and retrace your route back to the trailhead.

Camping: Guanella Pass Campground 2 miles east of the trailhead.

50 Grays and Torreys Peaks

Highlights: *A great outing up to the twin summits of Grays and Torreys Peaks. This strenuous hike reaches the summit of Grays Peak in 4-plus miles and 3,500 feet of elevation gain, and there is an option to climb Torreys Peak just to the west. Spectacular views, beautiful alpine peaks, and colorful summer wildflowers are what you can expect on this impressive alpine outing.*

Season: June to October.
Distance: 4.2 miles one way to the summit of Grays Peak.
Difficulty: Moderate to strenuous.
Maps: Trails Illustrated Idaho Springs/ Georgetown/Loveland Pass #104.
Management: Clear Creek Ranger District/ USDA Forest Service.

Trail conditions: The lower section of the trail is fairly smooth and well maintained. The upper section is steep, narrow, and rocky. Much work has been done on the upper section of the trail so stay on the trail and restrain from cutting switchbacks.

Finding the trailhead: From Denver follow Interstate 70 west to Georgetown. Travel 6.0 miles past Georgetown and exit the interstate at Bakerville. Cross over the interstate and follow Stevens Gulch Road for 3.0 miles south to the trailhead.

Key points:
2.0 Kiosk.
3.5 Trail junction.
4.2 Summit of Grays Peak.

The hike: From the trailhead cross Stevens Gulch Road and travel over a bridge to the start of the trail. Past the bridge the trail climbs at a modest grade up through dense willows on both sides of the trail. The trail hugs the eastern

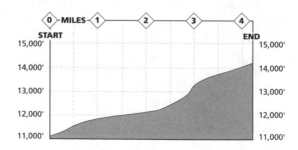

Grays and Torreys Peaks

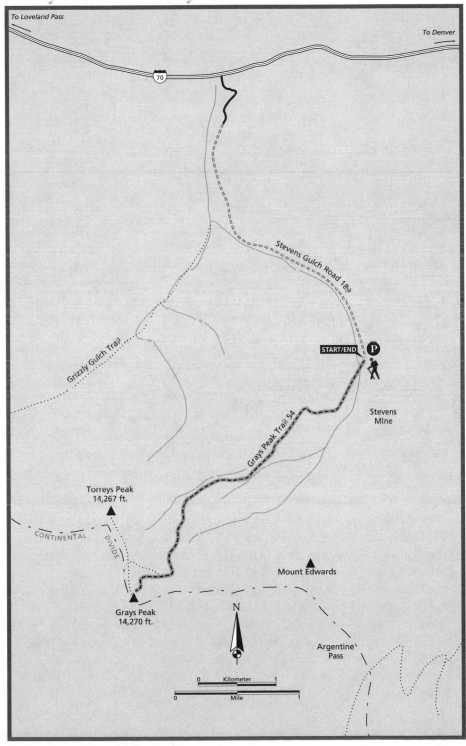

To Loveland Pass

To Denver

70

Stevens Gulch Road 189

Grizzly Gulch Trail

START/END P

Stevens Mine

Grays Peak Trail 54

Torreys Peak
14,267 ft.

CONTINENTAL   DIVIDE

Mount Edwards

Grays Peak
14,270 ft.

N

Argentine Pass

0   Kilometer   1

0   Mile   1

Grays Peak

flank of Kelso Mountain (13,164 feet) with spectacular views south to Mount Edwards and Grays and Torreys Peaks. Looking east, at the base of McClellan Mountain, one can see the remnants of the old Stevens Mine. The old decaying buildings and piles of tailings are all that remain of what was once the site of a large mining operation. At around the 2.0-mile mark reach a kiosk with trail information. This is a great place to take a short break before tackling the steep, strenuous hike ahead. Past the kiosk climb up through an often wet section into a large cirque below the impressive summits of Grays and Torreys Peaks. The trail cuts back to the east through a very rocky section and gains altitude very quickly. The hiking becomes laborious as you break out into open tundra following long switchbacks below the north face of Grays Peaks. Beautiful views open to Torreys Peak to the west and back down valley to

Kelso and McClellan Mountains. At around the 3.5-mile mark reach a trail junction and marker. The upper trail to the summit of Grays Peak used to be an old horse trail that carried tourists to the top of the mountain. The Colorado Fourteener Initiative made a number of improvements to the trail in the summer of 2001 and established logical trails to both summits. Going right will take you to a saddle between Grays and Torreys Peaks. Go left, following the switchbacks that steeply lead to the summit of Grays Peak. Reach the summit at around the 4.2-mile mark and enjoy spectacular views in all directions. This is why you climb a fourteener. You feel like you are standing on top of the world. Take a short break before retracing your route back to the trailhead.

Option: From the summit of Grays Peak follow the obvious ridgeline to the north. Reach a saddle between Grays and Torreys Peaks with a trail on the right. Continue up the ridge, quickly gaining the summit of Torreys Peak (14,267 feet) and your second fourteener in a day. Retrace your route back to the saddle and follow the trail back to the trailhead.

Note: These two peaks are considered to be easy fourteeners. Don't be fooled; they should demand your respect. Be prepared for rapid weather changes, lightning, hail, rain, or snow any time of the year. Bring a wind jacket or raincoat and extra clothing. Bring two quarts of water and food. The peaks see large hiker traffic during weekends in the summer months. Plan your trip during the week for a more enjoyable and peaceful experience. Plan an early start during the months of July and August to avoid thunderstorms, which can be extremely violent and scary. Plan on being off the summit by noon during these months.

South of Denver/
COLORADO SPRINGS AREA

51

Columbine Open Space

Highlights: *New open space and trails just south of Castle Rock. Two short trails just above Plum Creek and Interstate 25. The Columbine Open Space provides a buffer from the ever-encroaching growth along the I–25 corridor.*

Season: Year-round.
Distance: 2.6 miles for both loops.
Difficulty: Easy.

Maps: Douglas County/Columbine Open Space.
Management: Douglas County Open Space.
Trail conditions: Smooth.

Finding the trailhead: From Castle Rock travel south on I–25 to exit 174 (Tomah Road). Travel over the interstate and north on the Frontage Road (left) to the entrance of the Columbine Open Space. Follow the sign to the parking area and trailhead near a large red barn.

Key points:
0.2 Bench.
0.3 Start of the loop.
0.9 End of the loop.
1.3 Back at the trailhead and start of the north loop.
1.7 Start of the loop.
1.9 Bench.
2.2 End of the loop.
2.6 Back at the parking area.

The hike: This is a great little hike to get the young ones outdoors, so bring the kids along. From the parking area pass the kiosk and travel south on the wide path. Pass a bench and drop down a short hill to the start of the first loop. Go right and follow the wide path through an open area, with Plum Creek on the right, filled with willows and cottonwoods. The trail makes a sharp left and heads back north, with railroad tracks on your right. There are nice views to the north and west to Devils Head. Make a short climb back to the parking area and the start of the north loop. Pass the kiosk and follow the wide path across the road and down into an open area, with nice-looking cottonwoods and Plum Creek on the left. The trail makes a short climb and reaches a level area and bench. Go right and follow the trail, with railroad tracks on the right. Private property surrounds the trail, and the ever-expanding sprawl can be

Columbine Open Space

To Castle Rock

Plum Creek

25

frontage road

P

START/END

Glade Gulch

Tomah Road

exit 174

To Colorado Springs

N

| 0 | Kilometer | 0.5 |
| 0 | Mile | 0.5 |

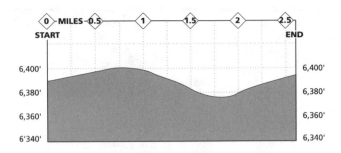

seen to the north. There are excellent views to the east and west. The trail curves back to the south and heads back to the trailhead. Retrace your route from the bench and soon arrive at the parking area. Be aware of the rattlesnake signs along the trail. Rattlesnakes like to sun themselves on the trail during the summer months. No dogs are allowed at Columbine Open Space.

52 Palmer Park

Highlights: *A fantastic hike through a city park with excellent views of Pikes Peak and the Garden of the Gods. Bizarre rock formations, wildflowers, and fields filled with blooming yuccas all contribute to an excellent hike within the city limits of Colorado Springs. There are many trails that crisscross Palmer Park. Follow the map and mileage cues and you shouldn't have any problems enjoying this beautiful area.*

Season: Year-round.
Distance: 5.7-mile loop.
Difficulty: Moderate.
Maps: City of Colorado Springs Parks and Recreation/Palmer Park.

Management: City of Colorado Springs.
Trail conditions: The trail varies from very smooth to extremely rocky.

Finding the trailhead: Travel south on Interstate 25 from Denver past the Air Force Academy to Academy Boulevard. Follow Academy Boulevard south to Maizeland Road. Turn right onto Maizeland Road and make a quick right into Palmer Park. Turn right into a large parking area near the ballparks. The hike starts here.

Palmer Park

Templeton Trail

Boy Scout camp

Edna Mae Nature Trail

Horse stable

Mesa Trail

Greencrest Trail

START/END
Ball fields

Maizeland Road

83

N

| 0 | Kilometer | 1 |
| 0 | Mile | 1 |

Key Points:

0.6 Greencrest Trail.

1.5 Road.

1.8 Parking area.

1.9 Templeton Trail.

2.5 Overlook.

3.0 Trail junction. Go left.

3.4 Junction with the North Canon Trail.

3.7 Junction with the Edna Mae Nature Trail.

3.9 Junction with Mesa Trail.

4.1 Yucca mesa.

4.2 Junction with Palmer Point Trail.

4.5 Road.

4.7 Greencrest Trail.

5.7 Back at the parking area.

The hike: From the parking area access the Greencrest Trail by going past
the northernmost baseball field and heading toward power lines at an old service road directly beyond centerfield. The Greencrest Trail is well marked and
follows the power lines on a wide dirt trail just east of the dog park. Follow the
Greencrest Trail past two private driveways and up through two picnic areas.
At around the 0.6 mile mark reach a trail junction. Follow the Greencrest Trail
up and right on a very rocky trail. The Greencrest Trail winds up past several
rock formations and gains a ridge. Follow the signs for the Greencrest Trail
and drop into an open meadow under the power lines. This is nice hiking
through a meadow filled with tall prairie grasses, yuccas, and scattered ponderosas; the trail leads you past a Boy Scout camp on the left and brings you to
a road at the 1.5-mile mark. Cross the road and reach the Palmer Crest Trail.
Go right on the Palmer Crest Trail on very narrow tread under the power
lines. The trail climbs up a short hill and then winds down to a large parking
area. Go left up past the restrooms and skirt the volleyball court to a junction
with the Templeton Trail. Go right on the Templeton Trail through thick

167

stands of Gambel oak to a trail junction. Go right following the Templeton Trail, heading north. The trail climbs through a very rocky section and reaches a high point with a strange rock formation on the right. Drop a short distance and then climb again on rocky tread, reaching an overlook. There are great views west to Pikes Peak and the red-colored cliffs of the Garden of the Gods. Past the overlook the trail drops down and cuts under the base of a large sandstone cliff. Beautiful hiking through this section leads you to a trail junction at the 3.0-mile mark. Go left and up on extremely rocky tread, hugging the base of large sandstone bluffs. Follow the rocky trail, with excellent views to the west, up to a trail junction at the 3.4-mile mark. Go right and down on the North Canon Trail and drop past several rock switchbacks to a parking area, horse stable, and the Edna Mae Nature Trail. Go left past the large trail sign onto the Edna Mae Nature Trail into a narrow gulch, climbing several rocky steps to a trail junction at the 3.9-mile mark. Go right at the trail marker leading up to the Mesa Trail and a large open mesa filled with yuccas. Head toward the east side of the mesa to a gate, road, and parking area. Access the trail across the road and go left at the trail marker on the Palmer Point Trail. The Palmer Point Trail parallels the road on nice smooth tread, and at the 4.5-mile mark crosses the road and then goes right through the ponderosas to a familiar junction with the Greencrest Trail. Follow the Greencrest Trail back to the parking area and the end of the hike.

53 Section 16/Palmer Trail

Highlights: *A beautiful and popular hike through the foothills west of Colorado Springs. An old growth pine forest, cool mountain streams, and spectacular vistas are the main attractions on this hike. You can hike this trail counterclockwise, but the description goes in a clockwise direction. Enjoy; this is one of the best hikes near Colorado Springs.*

Season: Year-round. Can be snowy in the winter months on the north-facing sections of the hike.
Distance: 5.8-mile loop.
Difficulty: Moderate.
Maps: Trails Illustrated Pikes Peak/Canon City #137.

Management: City of Colorado Springs Parks/Pike National Forest.
Trail conditions: Smooth for most of the hike. Rocky for the last 2.0 miles back to the trailhead.

Finding the trailhead: From Colorado Springs travel west on U.S. Highway 24 to 26th Street. Turn left on 26th Street and go to a four-way stop at Lower Gold Camp Road. Turn right onto Lower Gold Camp Road and travel 1.5 miles to the Section 16 Trailhead parking area on the right.

Key points:
0.3 High Drive.
0.9 Trail junction.
1.0 Palmer Trailhead.
1.2 Spur trail to old ruins.
2.7 Cross Hunter's Run.
3.3 Trail junction.
4.0 Go left.
4.9 Junction with Paul Intemann Trail.
5.8 Back at the parking area.

The hike: When I lived in Colorado Springs this used to be one of my favorite trail runs. I have run this trail at least a hundred times and must say I have enjoyed every one of those forays into the Hunter's Run drainage. The views are spectacular, wildflowers and yuccas bloom in the summer months, and the old growth pines are beautiful. From the parking area follow Lower Gold Camp Road (west) to High Drive. At the stop sign continue straight through a gate and follow High Drive, with Bear Creek on the right. The road and you climb at a steady rate past several rock formations on the steep hillsides. Bear Creek switches to the left at around the 0.6-mile mark. At around 0.9 mile look to the right for a trail coming straight out of a fence line. Ignore this trail and go a short distance up the road to the Palmer Trailhead at around the 1.0-mile mark. Turn right at an old metal gate onto the Palmer Trail and into a small open meadow. Follow the trail up to a junction at the 1.2-mile mark. Straight ahead lie the ruins of an old Boy Scout camp. You go right up a switchback and into the trees. The trail climbs steeply at first then recedes to a nice grade through the dense forest. The hiking is pretty straightforward, with the Hunter's Run drainage appearing down to the right. Occasional views through the pines to the east and south add to the overall beauty of the hike. The trail switches to the west side of the hill and then climbs past a rocky section, with views of the rocky Tenney Crags and Mount Arthur. The trail comes back to the east on a very narrow section and then meets beautiful Hunter's Run at the 2.7-mile mark. Do yourself a favor and take a short break at this beautiful mountain stream. Past the stream the trail cuts a narrow line across the steep hill and heads north up to a trail junction. There are great views south and east to Colorado Springs. Reach the trail junction and go right

Section 16/Palmer Trail

To Woodland Park

Manitou Springs

24

To Colorado Springs

26th Street

Paul Intemann Nature Trail

Lower Gold Camp Road

Palmer Trail

START/END

P

Hunter's Run

Four-way stop

Bear Creek

High Drive

N

| 0 | Kilometer | 1 |
| 0 | Mile | 1 |

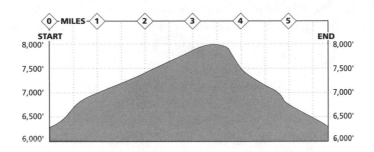

up to the high point of the hike. Enjoy the views across an open area, then dive back into the trees and arrive at a trail junction at the 4.0-mile mark. Go left and drop down the steep switchback to a section of very rocky and loose tread. The trail becomes quite steep and soon drops you into a small, open area with several spur trails. Go right, following the trail down through a rocky section to a junction with the Paul Intemann Nature Trail and level ground. At the Paul Intemann Nature Trail go right through the Gambel oak, with great views to a series of hogback ridges. The trail now has open views to the north of the Garden of the Gods Park. Travel down a series of steep switchbacks, where the trail ends abruptly at the parking area.

Paul Intemann Nature Trail

Highlights: *A great hike that starts just off Ruxton Avenue in downtown Manitou Springs. Beautiful views of Pikes Peak, Williams Canyon, and the Garden of the Gods Park. This is a year-round trail that sees a fair amount of foot and bike travel.*

Season: Year-round.
Distance: 2.7 miles one way.
Difficulty: Moderate.
Maps: Trails Illustrated Pikes Peak/Canon City #137.

Management: City of Manitou Springs.
Trail conditions: Lots of Pikes Peak pea gravel.

Finding the trailhead: From Interstate 25 and U.S. Highway 24 in Colorado Springs, travel west on US 24 to Manitou Springs. Travel through Manitou Springs to Ruxton Avenue. Go left on Ruxton Avenue for 1.5 miles to the trailhead on the left.

Key points:
0.1 Old service road.
0.2 Gate.
0.4 Bench and overlook.
0.6 Junction with the Red Mountain Trail.
1.1 Delaware Avenue.
1.4 Stone pillars.
1.7 Trail junction.
2.7 Crystal Park Cemetery.

The hike: From the parking area access the start of the Paul Intemann Nature Trail and head into the trees along a small creek. The trail crosses a small footbridge and quickly reaches an old service road. Go right on the road and climb to two metal posts with a chain going across the two posts. There is a sign marking the Paul Intemann Nature Trail by the left post. Go through the post and climb steeply up the loose gravel road. The trail is well marked and quickly turns east at a drainage on the right. Follow the old road, lined with yuccas and Gambel oak, up to a bench on the left at an overlook. Enjoy views to the east, west, and north to the Garden of the Gods. The trail climbs to a junction with the Red Mountain Trail on the right. Past the junction the trail drops down a series of steep steps to a wood footbridge. Cross the bridge and drop quickly to a road. Go left on the road and at the 1.4-mile mark go right past some pillars down into a small gulch. The trail then dumps you on Delaware Avenue. Follow Delaware Avenue, making a right at the 1.7-mile mark past a small playground. Follow the tight singletrack trail through stands

Paul Intemann Nature Trail

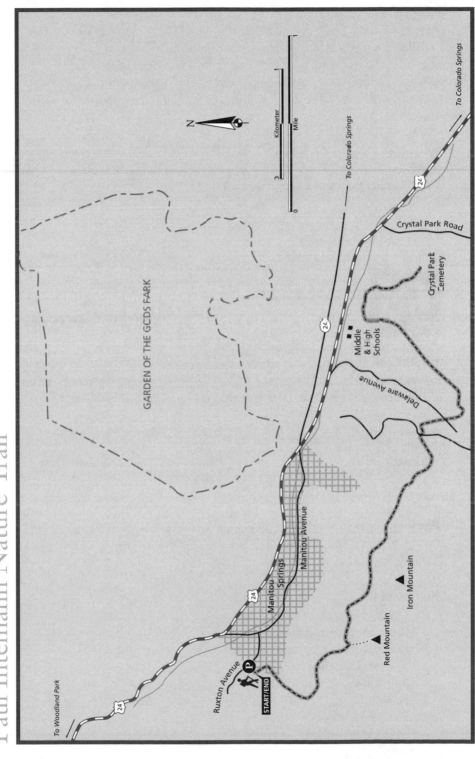

of pinion and juniper trees. The trail curves around the side of a steep hill, and Manitou Springs High School comes into view. The trail makes a sharp right, heading down toward the parking area. Skirt the parking area and climb on a narrow trail to the east. Look to the north for great views of the Garden of the Gods. The trail then heads south and drops down to the Crystal Park Cemetery and the end of the trail. Turn around and retrace your route back to the trailhead.

Manitou Springs is a wonderful place to visit and enjoy. There are many interesting shops along with a number of excellent restaurants, coffee shops, and bars. The town is very walker friendly and exploring the side streets is a great way to spend some time after your hike.

55   Waldo Canyon

Highlights: *A beautiful hike up into Waldo Canyon, with spectacular views of Colorado Springs, Pikes Peak, and Ute Pass. This is an extremely popular trail on the weekends. Plan on doing your hike midweek or in the early morning.*

Season: Year-round.
Distance: 7.0-mile loop.
Difficulty: Moderate.

Maps: Trails Illustrated Pikes Peak/Canon City #135.
Management: Pike National Forest.
Trail conditions: The trail can be rocky.

Finding the trailhead: From Colorado Springs take U.S. Highway 24 west up Ute Pass to Waldo Canyon. The parking area is on the right, 3.5 miles past Manitou Springs.

Key points:
0.1 Overlook and interpretive sign.
0.8 Ridge and view of Williams Canyon.
1.7 Sign and start of upper loop.
2.5 Stairs and trail junction.
4.9 Switchbacks.
5.3 Back at the sign.
7.0 Back at the stairs.

Waldo Canyon

To Woodland Park

Waldo Canyon Trail

START/END

Manitou Springs

N

0   Kilometer   1
0   Mile   1

24

To Colorado Springs

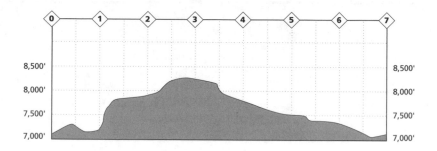

The hike: From the parking area climb up a series of steep steps to the start of the Waldo Canyon Trail. The trail becomes level and heads to the east past a registration box to an overlook on the right. Past the overlook and interpretive sign the trail heads north and contours around the side of a steep hill. Views open to the east to Colorado Springs and up and down Fountain Creek Canyon and US 24. The trail is wide and travels through an area of junipers, pinyon pines, Gambel oak, yuccas, mahogany oak, and cacti. The south-facing slope receives a lot of sun, and wildflowers thrive in the early summer months in the barren-looking, rocky soil. At around the 1.0-mile mark the trail gains a ridge and makes a left into Waldo Canyon. The trail drops for a short distance past several rocky sections. The narrow trail cuts across a steep slope through a dense forest of Douglas firs. Follow the trail, enjoying the shade of the tall trees, down into an open meadow past several campfire rings and campsites on the right. Reach a sign and small seasonal stream and the start of the Waldo Canyon upper loop. Take a short break and soak your feet in the cool waters of the stream. If you have the kids along and they are tired, this might be a good spot to turn around and head back to the parking area.

After a short rest take the left fork and follow the trail deep into Waldo Canyon, with the stream on the right. The trail is rocky and filled with roots. Ponderosas, Douglas firs, and blue spruce grow along with the occasional aspen and cottonwood. Water-loving wildflowers grow along the moist stream and are quite colorful during the summer months. The trail climbs at a steady pace and soon reaches a series of steep steps and a trail junction. The left trail heads west toward Cascade. The Waldo Canyon Trail goes right and climbs through a rocky section, gaining a ridge and the high point of the hike at 8,000 feet around the 3.0-mile mark. There are spectacular views south to the towering summit of Pikes Peak (14,110 feet) and down Waldo Canyon. The trail contours back to the east and south along a ridgeline. Leaving the ridge you begin a nice descent back into Waldo Canyon, curving back to the south, with open views of Pikes Peak, Cheyenne Mountain, Colorado Springs, and the plains. At around the 4.9-mile mark reach a series of steep switchbacks that drop you quickly back to the stream, the sign, and the end of the upper loop. Retrace your route, climbing gently out of Waldo Canyon, with views of the limestone cliffs of Williams Canyon and Pikes Peak, back to the parking area.

Appendix A
Resources

Barr Lake State Park
13410 Picadilly Road
Brighton, CO 80603
303 659 6005

Boulder Chamber of Commerce
2440 Pearl Street
Boulder, CO 80302
303–442–1044

Boulder Ranger District
2140 Yarmouth Avenue
Boulder, CO 80301
303–444–6600

Canyon Lakes Ranger District
1311 South College
Fort Collins, CO 80452
970–498–2770

City of Boulder Open Space
1300 Canyon Boulevard
Boulder, CO 80302
303–441–3400

Clear Creek Ranger District
101 Chicago Creek
P.O. Box 3307
Idaho Springs, CO 80452
303–567–3000

Colorado Springs Convention &
Visitors Bureau
515 South Cascade
Colorado Springs, CO 80903
719–635–7506 or 800–DO–VISIT

Colorado State Parks
1313 Sherman Street, #618
Denver, CO 80203
303–866–3437

Denver Metro Convention &
Visitor's Bureau
1555 California Street
Denver, CO 80202
303–892–1112

Eldorado Canyon State Park
P.O. Box B
Eldorado Springs, CO 80025
303–494–3943

Fort Collins Convention & Visitor's
Bureau
420 S. Howes Street, Suite 101
P.O. Box 1998
Fort Collins, CO 80522
970–482–5821

Golden Gate State Park
3873 Highway 46
Golden, CO 80403
303–583–3707

Horsetooth Mountain and
Reservoir Parks
Larimer County Parks Department
1800 S. County Road 31
Loveland, CO 80537
970–226–4517

Jefferson County Open Space
700 Jefferson County Parkway,
Suite 100
Golden, CO 80401
303–271–5925

Lory State Park
708 Lodgepole Drive
Bellevue, CO 80512
970–493–1623

Rocky Mountain National Park
1000 Highway 36
Estes Park, CO 80517
970–586–1206

South Platte District
19316 Goddard Ranch Court
Morrison, CO 80465
303–697–0414

Sulfur Ranger District
9 Ten Mile Drive
P.O. Box 10
Granby, CO 80446
970–887–4100

Appendix B
The Hiker's Checklist

Always make and check your own checklist!

If you've ever hiked into the backcountry and discovered that you've forgotten an essential, you know that it's a good idea to make a checklist and check the items off as you pack so that you won't forget the things you want and need. Here are some ideas:

Clothing
- Dependable rain parka
- Rain pants
- Windbreaker
- Thermal underwear
- Shorts
- Long pants or sweatpants
- Wool cap or balaclava
- Hat
- Wool shirt or sweater
- Jacket or parka
- Extra socks
- Underwear
- Lightweight shirts
- T-shirts
- Bandanna(s)
- Mittens or gloves
- Belt

Footwear
- Sturdy, comfortable boots
- Lightweight camp shoes

Bedding
- Sleeping bag
- Foam pad or air mattress
- Ground sheet (plastic or nylon)
- Dependable tent

Hauling
❏ Backpack and/or day pack

Cooking
❏ 1-quart container (plastic)
❏ 1-gallon water container for camp use (collapsible)
❏ Backpack stove and extra fuel
❏ Funnel
❏ Aluminum foil
❏ Cooking pots
❏ Bowls/plates
❏ Utensils (spoons, forks, small spatula, knife)
❏ Pot scrubber
❏ Matches in waterproof container

Food and drink
❏ Cereal
❏ Bread
❏ Crackers
❏ Cheese
❏ Trail mix
❏ Margarine
❏ Powdered soups
❏ Salt/pepper
❏ Main course meals
❏ Snacks
❏ Hot chocolate
❏ Tea
❏ Powdered milk
❏ Drink mixes

Photography
❏ Camera and film
❏ Filters
❏ Lens brush/paper

Miscellaneous
❏ Sunglasses
❏ Map and a compass
❏ Toilet paper
❏ Pocketknife
❏ Sunscreen

- ❏ Good insect repellent
- ❏ Lip balm
- ❏ Flashlight with good batteries and a spare bulb
- ❏ Candle(s)
- ❏ First-aid kit
- ❏ Your FalconGuide
- ❏ Survival kit
- ❏ Small garden trowel or shovel
- ❏ Water filter or purification tablets
- ❏ Plastic bags (for trash)
- ❏ Soap
- ❏ Towel
- ❏ Toothbrush
- ❏ Fishing license
- ❏ Fishing rod, reel, lures, flies, etc.
- ❏ Binoculars
- ❏ Waterproof covering for pack
- ❏ Watch
- ❏ Sewing kit

About the Author

Bob D'Antonio has spent many hours hiking, biking, and climbing throughout the United States. He has written several FalconGuides on mountain biking and rock climbing and is the author of *Hiking Colorado's Indian Peaks*. A native of Philadelphia, Pennsylvania, Bob lives in Louisville, Colorado, with his wife, Laurel, and their three children.